SCHIZOPHRENIA
a fresh approach

SCHIZOPHRENIA
a fresh approach

Gwen Howe

DAVID & CHARLES
Newton Abbot   London

This book is dedicated to the many schizophrenia sufferers I have met during the past sixteen years – some of the nicest and most courageous people I know.

British Library Cataloguing in Publication Data

Howe, Gwen
    Schizophrenia. – 2nd ed.
    1. Man. Schizophrenia
    I. Title
    616.8982

    ISBN 0-7153-9892-X

© Gwen Howe 1986
2nd edition 1990

Typeset by Typesetters (Birmingham) Ltd,
Smethwick, West Midlands
and printed in Great Britain
by A. Wheaton & Co Ltd, Hennock Road, Exeter
for David & Charles Publishers plc
Brunel House   Newton Abbot   Devon

Contents

Introduction

It is now four years since I wrote an introduction to the first edition of this book. It would be nice to think that during that time things had improved for people with schizophrenia and their families. Sadly, this is not the case. At present, 'community care' is an ideological concept rather than a reality for individuals who bear the scars of a serious mental illness. The suffering has merely been escalated by increasing difficulties in obtaining hospital beds in times of need.

What I wrote in my original introduction still stands. Many of those who suffer from schizophrenia can be protected from its worst horrors; those who become permanently and tragically disabled often do so after a second or third breakdown. Many such breakdowns are avoidable; they frequently occur because patients are unaware of the necessity to continue taking medication, often unaware, in fact, of their own diagnosis. If sufferers do not understand the nature of their illness, they have no chance of protecting themselves from further relapse and deterioration. If they do understand it, many contribute very positively to the sort of recovery that offers a reasonable quality of life. In some cases this can amount to a return to a normal lifestyle. However, there seems to be a growing reluctance in health professionals to take the responsibility for making and openly acknowledging this diagnosis, let alone offering explanations about what it means to the individual concerned.

Once again, I plead for all those who work with schizophrenia to take note that it is our squeamishness – not the patients' – that stops us taking preventative action and bringing this very common illness out into the open. *One in every one hundred of us* throughout the world will suffer with schizophrenia at some time during our lives. Why don't we accept it is part of the human condition; indeed, something that affects around one in every twenty-five families? I believe it is up to all of us to become more aware of this devastating illness, to recognise the early signs (and they are there for those who wish to see), and to act promptly and decisively so that we can protect its victims from avoidable and lasting despair.

Increasingly, the most tragic of those who have not been so protected can be found in the new 'cardboard cities' and in our overcrowded prisons. Community care will truly become a nightmare unless we act now.

I am so glad that many readers have found *Schizophrenia: A Fresh Approach* helpful. The number of sales and library borrowings has been very encouraging and I hope that this revised and updated edition will meet a continuing need. Finally, I must apologise to anyone who objects to my constant use of the word 'sufferer'. I do not find it acceptable to describe people as 'coeliacs' or 'diabetics' or 'schizophrenics', and feel it is more to the point to use the word 'sufferer' when discussing someone's particular disorder.

Gwen Howe
June 1990

PART I
What you need to know about the illness

1 What is Schizophrenia?

Although as many as 20 per cent of UK National Health Service hospital patients have this diagnosis, most people do not know what it is. Schizophrenia is one of the most serious and disabling illnesses known to humanity. It attacks nigh on one in every hundred people in all walks of life and in virtually all societies throughout the world. However, the official statistic of schizophrenia occurring in 1 per cent of the population is almost certainly an understatement, as doctors everywhere are most reluctant to use a diagnosis which will in itself have a drastic effect on the patient's future. The very word engenders fear in a society which has come to associate the illness with violence and shame. The mass media's apparent preoccupation with drama and scandal, together with professional secrecy, has contributed to this distortion of the truth. Doctors want to protect their patients; 'one-off' attacks are often labelled a 'nervous breakdown', 'adolescent disturbance' or 'post-natal depression'. At least some of the patients given such a diagnosis have in fact suffered a schizophrenic breakdown. If they are fortunate enough not to have a relapse, they will never be aware of this.

Meanwhile, any one of us may well have neighbours, workmates, friends and even relatives who, unbeknown to us, have suffered from schizophrenia. If they were identified, we would realise that there is nothing to fear or shun in this illness. Sadly, because of the secrecy surrounding schizophrenia, we sometimes seem to be a million light years away from such a healthy state of affairs!

It is widely believed that schizophrenia is a 'Jekyll and Hyde' syndrome. This is not the case; the misunderstanding may have arisen because the medical profession refers to a 'split mind'. This describes the process by which a patient's thoughts may become separated from his or her emotions; this does not actually occur in many patients and it has nothing to do with a 'dual personality', which is a very rare disorder.

Although stories reported in the mass media tend to associate schizophrenia with violence, many sufferers are timid, sensitive people.

Where there is violence, the diagnosis of schizophrenia is often secondary to a severe personality disorder. The exceptions are those cases in which effective treatment and support have not been provided and patients are out of touch with reality and tortured by their symptoms. Most of the ensuing tragedies could, and should, be avoided; all make news. Not so, the plight and the triumphs of the vast majority of victims of the illness!

Who are these individuals? They are, in the first instance, ordinary young people usually in their teens or early twenties. The vast majority of cases occur around times of hormonal change; for example, following puberty, after childbirth and after the menopause. Female patients often suffer worse symptoms at times of, and just before, menstrual periods.

It seems likely that the diagnosis of schizophrenia covers several conditions and describes a cluster of symptoms which are classic to the illness but which may, nevertheless, spring from varying causes. Attempts have been made to categorise the illness, and textbooks have usually referred to four main divisions: simple, hebephrenic, catatonic and paranoid.

According to this analysis, 'simple' schizophrenia is the form of the illness that creeps up insidiously and almost imperceptibly in an already withdrawn young person, probably from a family with a history of the illness. It used to be suggested that the prognosis was poor in such a case and that the patient was unlikely to become well enough to live a normal life. The term 'hebephrenic' schizophrenia was used to describe the more sudden-onset illness with all of the 'bizarre' symptoms, again often in a young person, but this time with a previously more stable personality. The outlook was thought to be much brighter in this case. 'Catatonia' describes, rather confusingly, two very different symptoms; on the one hand, there is the mute patient who can hold a bizarre statue-like pose for hours on end, with every appearance of unconsciousness and, on the other hand, the patient who is abnormally active and excited. 'Paranoid' schizophrenia describes the form of the illness in which the patient suffers from delusions and may be persecuted by voices which torment and deride, both contributing to, and aggravating, the individual's belief that the world has become very hostile.

Less emphasis is placed on this type of classification nowadays and this is not really surprising as it does not seem to be particularly useful. Prognosis is rarely as simple as suggested and, in any event, it is not so unusual to observe all the varied symptomatology in one patient over a period of time. Perhaps equally confusing is the division made between the so-called 'acute' and 'chronic' forms of the illness. The problem with this classification is that some patients may be described as being chronically ill because they suffer intermittent relapses or have to rely on medication indefinitely. However, in such cases, the illness may manifest itself only in its 'acute' form, with little resemblance to the symptoms and handicap associated with the 'chronic' form of schizophrenia.

It is probably more helpful to use the categories 'positive' symptoms and 'negative' symptoms to describe the two forms of the illness sometimes referred to as 'acute' and 'chronic'. 'Positive' symptoms are those which usually respond quite dramatically to medication and these include delusions, hallucinations and pronounced thought disorder. There will be a detailed discussion on symptoms in the next chapter, but for now it will suffice to equate 'positive' symptoms with all the 'bizarre' behaviour that usually accompanies an acute relapse or breakdown. These sorts of symptoms may disappear as suddenly as they came, but more usually this will happen gradually over a long period, and the eventual outlook for the future may well be bright. 'Negative' symptoms are those which seem to be largely unaffected by medication. The mood is flat and the patient is unresponsive and seemingly unemotional, perhaps retarded in reaction, and quite unable to cope with normal socialising. This form of the illness may be irreversible, although improvement can certainly be achieved. It usually creeps up insidiously on the individual, but it has been observed that some patients slip into this category after several breakdowns of the 'acute' type.

Crow and colleagues[1] have suggested that it might be helpful to refer to Type I and Type II syndromes, with Type I equating with 'positive' symptoms as described above and Type II equating with 'negative' symptoms. They do not see these as separate diseases, particularly as Type I can often progress into Type II syndrome. They associate Type I with an increase in dopamine receptors (to be discussed in some detail in Chapter 3) and Type II with cell loss and structured changes in the brain. Importantly, therefore, one syndrome seems to be concerned with malfunctioning and the other with actual organic change.

Clearly, it has not been easy to reach any definite conclusions over a definition of schizophrenia and this is not really surprising. Richter points out that: 'the present position is that schizophrenia is currently recognised as a term applied to a group of similar, but by no means identical, mental illnesses.'[2] There is, however, complete agreement that this illness is a psychosis. Mental illness is divided into two divisions: neurotic and psychotic disorders. Neurosis is relatively common and, thus, familiar. To an extent everyone has some element of neurosis in their personality; many of us have irrational fears of spiders, snakes or mice for instance. These are 'phobias' and, so long as they do not prevent us functioning properly, they are of little consequence in our lives. Another form of neurosis is 'obsessional' behaviour and, again, it is a question of the severity of this trait that determines whether or not the individual is actually ill. For example, the 'house-proud' wife is often efficient, energetic and well-motivated to do her work well; it is only if she insists on persevering repetitively with this work at the expense of more important matters that it becomes clear that an obsession is preventing her from functioning properly. At its worst, this sort of behaviour can result in continual cleaning and hand-washing in an attempt to eliminate unseen germs. Similarly, a phobia can result in the individual being unable to travel by public transport or, even, afraid to leave the home. These, then, are typical neurotic conditions.

Few of us know so much about the other major form of mental illness – psychosis. There are two main types of psychotic illness; one is the bi-polar form of depression we call manic depressive illness and the other, much more common, is schizophrenia. During a psychotic phase, the patient loses touch with reality at least some of the time and is usually quite unaware that he or she is ill. This is the main difference, then, between neurosis and psychosis. In the former, the patient is painfully aware of the problem, although this insight does not necessarily contribute to recovery. In the latter, the patient suffers acute symptoms but is not aware these are caused by illness; ironically, insight in this case would lead to treatment and, in most cases, remission of symptoms.

This leads us to the controversial area of medication in mental illness. In neurosis, this usually consists of drugs intended to allay some of the anxiety underlying the disorder. One group of such drugs – the minor tranquillisers – have been widely over-prescribed by GPs and it is understandable that this has led to public outcry. However, whereas neurosis may not respond to drug treatment, there is no doubt at all that psychosis not only responds to it, but that at the present time we have very little in the way of alternative treatment. The drugs that are specific to the treatment of schizophrenia are sometimes called 'major tranquillisers' and this has led to some confusion. In fact, the anti-psychotic drugs are *not* tranquillisers in the sense we mean when we talk about drugs like Valium and Librium and other 'minor tranquillisers'. The medication used in schizophrenia has a specific, and as yet little understood, effect on the chemistry of the brain and corrects certain abnormalities in functioning. Although this action certainly does alleviate the nightmarish experiences of a psychotic breakdown, it does not sedate the patient in any other way; more usually, it actually invigorates the individual and dispels some of the disabling lethargy caused by the illness.

The dramatic effect of chemicals on schizophrenia points to there being a physical origin to this type of mental illness. This is not as strange as it sounds; we already have examples of this sort of phenomenon in an illness such as pellagra – now known to be caused by a severe vitamin B_3 deficiency – and in vitamin B_{12} and folic acid deficiency. An imbalance in the body's chemistry leads to a detrimental effect on the brain and this in turn causes abnormalities in thought, perception and behaviour. For many years during this century, medical attention has focused rather more on the resultant behaviour changes and distorted relationships in schizophrenia than on the disease itself and Hoffer has described this as 'the flight from the medical model'.[3] As this has achieved nothing in terms of alleviating the symptoms of the illness but has led to a considerable increase in the suffering of those caring for the patient, it is indeed good news that the 'medical model' seems to be coming back into fashion again (the reader will find a more detailed discussion in Chapter 3).

What other factors point to schizophrenia being a *physical* disease? It is common for patients to have a background of digestive complaints of one sort or another. In a survey conducted by the Schizophrenia Association of Great Britain, 108 out of 253 patients had suffered with these. Early feeding difficulties were common and there was a frequent occurrence of unexplained bouts of sickness and 'gut' problems. It is becoming clear that some patients suffer from food and chemical allergies and that contact with these allergens provokes the return of psychotic symptoms. Research is under way at the time of writing to investigate the incidence of coeliac disease in families with schizophrenia; a connection that has been observed by other investigators. Before tuberculosis was controlled, schizophrenic patients used to be particularly vulnerable to developing the disease and many died of it. In contrast, it is rare to find sufferers who develop rheumatoid arthritis and some patients are clearly oblivious to physical pain. They are also better able to withstand surgical shock.

It is now generally accepted that schizophrenia has a genetic component (for further discussion of this, see Chapter 3); however, the incidence of the illness is high for a genetically determined disorder. This has intrigued several researchers and Richter comments:

> A detrimental gene responsible for a serious illness such as schizophrenia would be gradually eliminated from the population by the normal processes of natural selection unless it was associated with some favourable characteristic.[4]

He goes on to mention that earlier investigators have noted a high incidence of mental illness in men of genius and in their families, and recently

Karlsson found the incidence of schizophrenia to be considerably higher in the near relatives of a large group of distinguished writers, poets and scholars than in the general population.[5]

This researcher concluded that creative ability might be the favourable characteristic associated with the schizophrenic gene. Certainly, it is very common to find patients who have enormous creative ability. It is also common to find they have youthful good looks and an appearance very much younger than their chronological age!

Carter and Watts[6] report a possible protection from viruses in the families of schizophrenic patients and this may well be another advantage contributing to the survival and persistence of the disorder. However, whatever the role of this gene might be in the evolution of mankind, there can be no doubt that the cost is much too high for the individual sufferer. Let us look at some statistics that bear this out.

About a quarter of all patients recover more or less completely after one breakdown. Another 10 per cent become so damaged that after one or two breakdowns they are quite unable to survive outside of a hospital-type setting. In between those two extremes, the majority of sufferers have to battle with symptoms that are ever present or threatening to be so. At any time there are some 35,000 people with the illness in hospital, 2,500 in hostels or other dwellings and between 60 and 70,000 attending out-patient clinics or getting some day care.[7] Less than half of men with schizophrenia marry. Rather more women do, but their divorce and separation rates are well above the average. There is a high rate of suicide in patients with the illness and it may be higher than realised; there is almost always a considerable delay in diagnosis and one wonders how many student suicides are caused by schizophrenia as they occur at a time when the illness frequently strikes down its victims. Finally, and tragically, over half of all cases start between the ages of sixteen and thirty-five years of age, with the highest onset for men being in the late teens or early twenties; a time of hope and endeavour for most people.

The rest of Part I of this book will concentrate on the peculiarities of this tantalising disease, before we go on to discuss ways of tackling these problems and alleviating unnecessary stress. Meanwhile, let us leave it to the National Schizophrenia Fellowship to sum up these difficulties:

> Wherever it occurs ignorance about its causation and the absence of a cure interact with the dread and revulsion which still surround the disorder to create both a uniquely painful family situation and a complex community problem.[8]

In the next chapter we shall look at the sort of symptoms that are experienced by sufferers.

2 What are the Symptoms?

What do we know about the symptoms of schizophrenia? The onlooker can only perceive signs rather than symptoms and it is a remarkable fact that a relative or friend can live through a seemingly endless nightmare and become almost unrecognisable before you suspect that he or she is ill. Why is this?

The main reason for this phenomenon is the insidious onset of the illness, which creeps up on its victim so slowly that even in retrospect it is difficult to determine when it started. Another reason is that schizophrenia often attacks young people in the mid and late teens, with most sufferers diagnosed by their early twenties. This is a time of change and development and it is normal for a young person to become more sensitive, to become preoccupied with finding and establishing his or her identity and to become more liable to unexplained outbursts. This is part of adolescence; a vigorous effort to find one's own level in the outside world and to break away from dependence upon one's family. Many parents are perplexed and concerned about the behaviour of their *normal* offspring at this stage. They will be acutely aware of the 'generation gap' and the young person will alternate exasperatingly between almost stubborn independence on the one hand and the vulnerability of a young child on the other. Just to add to the confusion, he or she may be going through the agonising throes of first, or unrequited love, and be not really aware of the existence of anyone else in the household!

If this is the typical state of affairs in the normal adolescent's household, why should the parents of the unfortunate youngster destined to contract a devastating illness be alarmed when he or she becomes more solitary and withdraws from previously enjoyed social activities? It is quite understandable that the youngster may become suddenly rather shy and quiet, possibly tentative about relationships with the opposite sex; it is quite natural for an adolescent to spend hours in the privacy of the bedroom, playing records or sitting staring into space; nor is it unusual either to be immersed in studies, or to lose interest in them and fail to maintain previous standards of work. A parent may feel qualms even at this stage, but that is all part of being a parent. Every stage of development in one's offspring raises some anxiety until they come through each successfully! Meanwhile, any doubts voiced will be calmed by more objective onlookers, who will find quite reasonable explanations for changed behaviour in the young person. Any attempt to probe or challenge at this stage will certainly achieve nothing; the young person will become more defensive and less approachable, as would any of his or her peers!

By the time that parents are realising that their son or daughter has changed significantly, other signs should be evident. One tell-tale one may well be insomnia; the young person will show little inclination to retire to bed at the normal time. Many a mother has lain awake at night, wondering why her supposedly healthy son or daughter cannot sleep, as he or she roams around the house or plays records most of the night, only to fall into a stupor around dawn and have to be dragged out of bed in the morning. Another sign may be an apparent craving for junk foods, in particular 'stodge', and endless cups of tea or coffee. These will probably be preferred to 'proper' meals and the young person's table manners may reach an 'all time low'. On the other hand, he or she may avoid family meals altogether, apparently acutely self-conscious about eating with others and snatching junk-food 'tit-bits' day and night instead.

Yet another sign may be a marked indifference about hygiene and personal appearance; this is very suspect, as young people care deeply about these things, which are so important to self-image and popularity with peers. However studiedly casual the dress, considerable effort goes into carefully achieving this effect, as most families know!

What initially seemed to be rather withdrawn behaviour may now develop into marked *avoidance* behaviour. The young person will manage to disappear whenever visitors come into the home and there will be a significant lack of social contact outside the home too. Temper tantrums may develop into outbursts of wild accusations, which make no sense at all to the family. The young person may even use indescribably bad language that is completely out of character with his or her background – and I *do* mean indescribably bad language!

Finally, the individual will probably be relating exclusively to one person by now – usually his or her mother, but not always. The chosen 'prop' will very soon wonder at the intensity of this dependent relationship and at the same time be perplexed at the sufferer's ability to remain distant and aloof. It is perhaps the abnormal content of this relationship, and the inappropriateness of a dependence reminiscent of a very young child's, that finally convinces a mother – she is usually the first to insist that something is wrong – that the young person is ill. Meanwhile, it should have become quite clear by now that the individual's personality has undergone a dramatic change, but so slowly! (For a detailed discussion about obtaining help, see Chapter 7.)

Meanwhile, what has been happening to the young person? What are the symptoms which have produced these changes? All sorts of alarming experiences happen in schizophrenia. Let us consider some of these, remembering that everyone is unique and that the illness affects different people in different ways.

The underlying theme of all patients' symptoms seems to be a restless anxiety which gradually erodes the individual's confidence. Feelings of guilt intrude on all his or her thoughts and actions, however innocent these may be, and it is not at all uncommon for the individual to come to believe that he or she is worthless and, later, evil. There is usually no basis whatsoever for such judgements but, as you will see, some of the classic symptoms of the illness contribute to such harrowing ideas.

Patients often have delusional ideas and the reader will understand these better if reminded of the oft-mentioned phrase 'delusions of grandeur' which we use to indicate that some people have elevated opinions of themselves. Patients may believe they are God, Joan of Arc or some other divine or famous person. On the other hand, they may have delusions of the guilt-ridden variety; they may believe they are responsible for all the evils in the world, or, more specifically, for the latest disaster reported in the mass media. Delusions may be concerned with the body; they may be convinced that their brain is dissolving, or that muscles or bones are wasting away. Sometimes there are delusions about money, with the individual convinced that financial disaster looms around the corner. Some schizophrenic patients, living in the community, have been known to deprive themselves of heating in mid-winter and, worse, of food, in their determination to hang on to every penny. All sorts of hypochondriacal delusions may be present and patients are often terrified that they have contracted a fatal physical illness. Others are convinced that a loved one is in danger and that this is in some way the fault of the sufferer.

Even more common than these sort of delusional ideas are hallucinations, and the auditory type probably cause as much misery and confusion to patients as most other symptoms put together. These vary from mutterings and whisperings to voices shouting abuse at the indvidual. The schizophrenic patient hears things that are not there; note that I say '*hears* things' and not '*imagines* hearing things'. We do not yet know what sort of mechanism allows this to happen; it is as if some sort of 'short-circuiting' takes place and the brain receives inaccurate messages. Suffice it to say that these messages reflect the shattered self-image of the individual. Sometimes the patient suspects he or she is listening to his or her own thoughts and will say 'I think I am hearing my own thoughts!' somewhat apologetically. Such an experience is possibly much easier to live with and, importantly, to rationalise, than the sound of a voice calling one's name and shouting instructions or unkind names.

And what about the voice or voices that are heard discussing the individual in the third person? What about the voices of loved ones which are heard criticising the sufferer, perhaps cursing, perhaps planning to kill him or her? The cruel irony here is that the individual developing the illness is not aware that his or her senses are playing tricks in this way and life becomes a nightmare in which the very people one loves have become two-faced and, it seems, one's enemies. Small wonder that the individual grows hostile and secretive within the shelter of his or her own home.

Not every sufferer will experience such hallucinations, but I believe it to be important for relatives and friends to keep the possibility in mind. Sometimes even professionals overlook the fact that patients may be quite oblivious to the fact that they have experienced such a symptom. How does one know one has experienced a hallucination if in fact this has fitted, however agonisingly, into the apparent reality of everyday life? The patient is in a similar situation to the person who is colour blind and unaware of it. He or she is merely painfully aware that formerly trusted loved ones deride or hate the sufferer and when doctors talk of 'hearing voices', this is innocently denied. I have known instances where the medical team has remained unaware of the reasons for a patient's hostility towards the family and, accordingly, unaware of his or her auditory hallucinations. This leaves the recovering patient without a rationalisation for things heard and it puts the family at a sad disadvantage, unable to heal the patient's hurt and to provide the supportive environment needed for recovery. (For a detailed discussion on coping with this sort of dilemma, see Chapter 8.)

Auditory hallucinations, then, are common. Mutterings, or perhaps music, may be heard, but it is more usual for the patient to hear voices. These may give all sorts of instructions, the most dangerous sort being 'Don't take your medication', 'Don't believe them', or 'You must kill yourself.' Needless to say, these symptoms are the most worrying and it is reassuring to note that they usually respond well to neuroleptic drug treatment. At the very least, auditory hallucinations provide yet more harassment and stress to a bewildered sufferer; at worst, they can be destructive to relationships and sometimes to life itself.

Visual hallucinations are less common; these, as the name suggests, involve seeing things which are not there. This may be a ghost or perhaps the flashing of lights. Some patients believe they have experienced a visitation from God and this, not unnaturally, has a profound effect on their ideas and beliefs henceforth.

Another strange experience which happens to many sufferers is the conviction that all communications are in some way concerned with them. Patients frequently feel that the announcer or newsreader on the television, for example, is talking to them, or about them. The news being relayed over the air has a special meaning and it is clear to the individual that he or she is being discussed. It is not surprising, therefore, that some sufferers studiously avoid the television or radio – this can be another tell-tale sign that something may be wrong. Similarly, conversations going on around the individual, or non-verbal signals – such as the rubbing of a hand, the wiping of a forehead, the tapping of a foot – are believed to be part of a message about the sufferer, with everyone else aware of this. Here we see yet another piece of the jig-saw in the paranoid picture and have further insight into yet more reasons for any hostility shown by the tortured individual. Even when 'voices' are not in evidence, patients complain that others are involved in 'double-talk' and that secret messages are understood by everyone else.

It is not surprising, therefore, that some patients are convinced that others can read their thoughts and predict their next actions. Some feel that they are being influenced and controlled by others and these sort of sensations and beliefs are part of the feelings of loss of identity that patients may experience. It is as if the boundary separating the individual from others becomes muzzy and the individual's personality merges with the rest. This is a frightening sensation and one that leads to beliefs of omnipotence in world affairs, for example, or, alternatively, feelings of helplessness and being controlled in some way.

We have already remarked on the sufferer's ability to stay awake all night and to be lethargic and sleep all day; this is a very common symptom. There may be other apparent changes in the perception of time. Some patients experience the sensation that time stands still and there will be no tomorrow; this slowing up of time often accompanies depressive illnesses, and it will be no surprise to learn that schizophrenic sufferers may become very depressed. Many patients can sit for hours and hours at a time, staring into space, and be quite unaware of the time passing. Delusional ideas sometimes relate to perceptions of time and patients may be convinced that they are living in another age, perhaps an earlier decade in their lifetime. They may gather around them clothes and records which relate to that time.

Schizophrenia is an illness that produces distorted perception, and all five senses – hearing, sight, taste, touch and smell – may be affected. What, in fact, does this mean?

Let us consider hearing first. Sounds may be too loud, or too high-pitched, so that the individual becomes acutely sensitive to any noise. The healthy person 'selects' relevant stimuli; we hear only those things which we are 'tuned' into. For example, we may listen to a friend's chatter, but not notice bird-song outside or the drone of distant traffic. The schizophrenic sufferer may be unable to select in this way. All sounds will intrude with equal intensity and the individual is bombarded with noise, unable to concentrate on one thing at a time. Just consider what a daunting challenge ordinary conversation must be under these circum-stances!

Hallucinations are also part of the distorted perceptions and these have already been discussed in relation to hearing and sight. Other visual distortions may be the judging of distance and the space we all like around ourselves. It is not uncommon for the schizophrenic patient to offend by projecting his or her face too near to the faces of others in conversation. Patients may be misunderstood if they move up too close to a member of the opposite sex, who may see this as aggressive or provocative behaviour. Shapes may change; people may look funny and lopsided or change their usual form, animals may become too large and, therefore, threatening. Colours may be too vivid, as in a poor techni-colour film or, alternatively, everything may seem grey or black or colourless.

Perhaps the most far-reaching disturbance in visual perception is the impaired ability to assess whether others are watching one. It seems that many patients are acutely aware of being watched; they believe that others are staring at them all the time and this sensation is yet another part of the paranoid picture. Perhaps for this reason, sufferers find it very difficult to maintain eye contact with others. One patient has described the sensation of staring into another's eyes as equivalent to receiving an electric shock!

Another factor contributing to paranoia is the bitter taste that patients associate with food and drink. This leads to the conviction, not unreasonably, that their food has been 'doctored' and they are being poisoned.

The sense of touch can also be distorted, with, for example, smooth substances feeling furry and 'three dimensional'. More commonly, some patients may feel a sensation of 'creepy' skin, or that their insides are being tampered with. This leads to some of them believing that another person, creature or spirit has entered their bodies; religious ideas sometimes figure in this and the patient may believe Christ has entered his or her body. Similarly, some patients believe their sexual identity has been changed in some way and unfounded fears of homosexuality are common.

The sense of smell can be heightened considerably; some sufferers claim they can smell others and they insist that those around them bath more often! Others can smell their own bodies and assume that those around them are aware of this odour. This, naturally, is very distressing.

Summing up, then, all five senses can become acutely sensitive and, at the same time, false messages are being relayed to the individual. It is not too difficult to understand why a personality can be shattered by this illness; all the sufferer's past experiences and learning can be rendered null and void. Messages are now being received that make nonsense of the individual's previous understanding of the world. Amidst a barrage of unwanted stimuli, the brain is desperately trying to rationalise all these experiences and here we have a very likely explanation of the delusions and paranoia which are so common a feature of the illness. The individual frantically tries to sort out all these strange messages and produces equally strange, but often appropriate, explanations. Such is the stuff of survival; if the individual cannot make some sort of 'sense' out of what is happening, then all is lost. Small wonder that he or she comes up with all sorts of strong convictions and is impervious to others' objections to their foundation. Small wonder that many of these convictions seem strange to those of us fortunate enough to live much simpler lives.

These, then, are some of the bizarre experiences that may have been happening to the sufferer. To return to the start of this discussion, it is important not to overlook the fact that any or many of these symptoms will be occurring against a backcloth of uncertainty, acute self-consciousness and distorted feelings of guilt. These last three feelings are more in keeping with our own experiences; we can understand rather better the pain these can cause and we should be able to recognise this pain. If you see your child/relative in distress, do something about it! All the other symptoms may escape your attention or understanding, but we all recognise unhappiness and we sense when this becomes something more like desperation. (For a detailed discussion on obtaining help, you may like to refer to Chapter 7 at this stage.)

Meanwhile, we have discussed at some length the sort of symptoms that may be experienced by someone contracting this illness. Rather different symptoms may be experienced by sufferers who become chronically ill (see Chapter 1 for a discussion on the acute and chronic forms of schizophrenia). In the chronic form of the illness, it is not unusual for the patient to seem very flat emotionally. He or she may seem unmoved, to a great extent, by the joy or suffering of others and seem to be too self-absorbed to care about these things. This introspection may well be due to the barrage of over-stimulation of the mind; the patient seems withdrawn and 'switched off', but it is very probable that this is a defence mechanism to protect him or her from yet more harassment.

Perhaps for the same sort of reason, the patient will find ordinary conversation excruciatingly difficult, particularly the small-talk our society indulges in so happily. In all probability, the individual will find it quite impossible to initiate conversation at any time.

Apathy (lack of motivation to do anything), inability to concentrate and extreme lethargy are all common in the chronic form of the illness. There may be impairment of intellectual ability and a general slowing-up in reaction and reflexes. The patient looks unwell and medical professionals will often recognise the typical appearance of a patient with chronic schizophrenia. All these symptoms are described as 'negative-type' symptoms, as against the 'positive-type' symptoms described earlier, but patients with this form of the illness may have some of these latter symptoms and may also suffer 'acute' relapses at times. The positive-type symptoms are those which very often respond quite dramatically well to the neuroleptic drugs. However, up to now, no really effective treatment has been found for the negative-type symptoms.

Physical symptoms can occur with both forms of the illness and these are quite common. Lethargy and physical exhaustion are commonly found in other diseases, but they are a prominent feature in schizophrenia. Patients often complain bitterly of aches and pains, particularly in the stomach or the lower limbs. They often look physically ill, with an extreme pallor and loss of weight. It is common for the menstrual cycle in women to be interrupted and monthly periods may be absent for some time, only to return as the disease wanes. There may be an escalation of allergic-type conditions with the onset of an acute attack, with a sudden worsening of the patient's allergic rhinitis, for example, or asthma.

These, then, are some of the symptoms of this illness, but not all. Schizophrenia has been described as a 'living death'. Certainly, it can alienate the sufferer from all those around him or her; to most of us, that sort of isolation would indeed seem to be a living death. In the next chapter we will discuss possible causes of this extraordinary illness.

3 What are the Causes?

Perhaps the title of this chapter is misleading inasmuch as it may convey the idea that the causes of schizophrenia have been established. Unfortunately, this is not the case. Much effort, goodwill and frustration have been spent in searching for the reasons for this illness. Some quite extraordinary ideas – that is, extraordinary to those of us armed with mere common sense rather than expertise – have been given credit along the way; but just for brief periods, mercifully! One such idea – highly unlikely to anyone familiar with the misery caused by psychosis – was that the sufferer was the sane member of an otherwise sick society, who had opted out into a happier world. Another was that schizophrenia, together with other mental illnesses, was a myth. Let us look at some other theories that have proved rather longer lasting.

It had seemed highly probable ever since the first research in genetics back in 1916 that schizophrenia has a hereditary basis. Results of studies at that time, and since, have led one researcher – Kety – to remark 'If schizophrenia is a myth, it is a myth with a strong genetic component.'[1] In 1938, Kallman[2] conducted a study in Germany that involved a very large sample of 13,851 people and he found a significantly increased risk of schizophrenia in first-degree relatives of a sufferer. Although the evidence was fairly convincing, enthusiasts of the environmental school (those convinced that upbringing is all-important) pointed out that these findings could merely confirm their own theories that this devastating disease is caused by faulty child-rearing. This sort of criticism led to further genetic studies, this time with twins; it was believed that these could disentangle the 'nature versus nurture' argument once and for all. There are two types of twins; monozygotic (MZ) twins are identical and share exactly the same genes, having been formed by the splitting into two of one fertilised egg. Dizygotic (DZ) twins are formed in two separate eggs from two sperm cells and they therefore share half of their genes only, as do other brothers and sisters. All are usually brought up in the same environment, so a stronger correlation between MZ twins would indicate a stronger genetic component in the illness. Kallman undertook this type of research,[3] this time in the USA, in 1946, and he studied 60 MZ twins and 276 DZ twins. He found a 65 per cent concordance rate (that is, where one twin had contracted schizophrenia, the other also became ill) for the MZ twins. He found an 8 per cent concordance for the DZ twins and this correlated approximately with other findings for risks for brothers and sisters. In 1953, Slater[4] considered all schizophrenic admissions between 1936 and 1950 in hospitals in the London area. He found a 68 per cent concordance rate in 41 MZ twins and an 11 per cent concordance rate for the 115 DZ twins. These results were impressively similar to the earlier study on twins and later research has replicated the findings. However, critics in the environmental school continued to challenge the results and, accordingly, the research became more and more sophisticated. Finally, 'adoption' and 'fostering' studies have confirmed all the previous findings that there is indeed an important genetic component in this illness.[5,6,7,8,9]

Unfortunately, the type of gene involved has escaped detection up to the present time. This is a pity, as its discovery would make it possible to predict risk and would make for effective counselling for would-be parents. What we do know is that, generally, the following rules apply:

1. Most schizophrenia sufferers are born to non-schizophrenic parents.
2. Members of the general population have a 1 per cent chance of becoming schizophrenic.
3. If you have an uncle, aunt, niece or first cousin with schizophrenia, then you have a 2–3 per cent chance of contracting it.
4. If you have one parent, brother or sister with the illness, you have up to a 10 per cent chance of developing it yourself.
5. If you have two parents who have schizophrenia, then you have about a 40 per cent chance of developing it.
6. If your MZ twin has schizophrenia, then you have a 60 per cent chance of developing the illness, the risk decreasing with age.

These figures, and particularly those for MZ twins, make it clear that other factors are operating as well as genetics. Something in the individual's environment is tipping the balance. One theory has been concerned with social class and poverty; however, although there is a disproportionate number of schizophrenia sufferers in areas associated with poverty, it seems highly probable that this phenomenon reflects the sad results of a disability that renders its most handicapped victims unable to hold down employment and perform accepted social skills. As mentioned in Chapter 1, schizophrenia attacks people of all classes and creeds.

Another theory is concerned with stress, which is, of course, a factor aggravating any illness. However, the incidence of schizophrenia has persisted through good times and bad and in all types of culture, some much more exposed to stress than others. In recent times it has even been noted that first-time admissions to hospital decreased in war-ridden Europe in the 1940s, despite adequate medical facilities.[10] All in all, there is no evidence to suggest that stress, in the environmental sense, is a factor which predisposes the genetically vulnerable individual to *develop* schizophrenia, although it is certainly possible that stress can contribute to relapse in patients with a poor prognosis. There is no reason why the unsuccessful search for the missing environmental factor should be seen as leading inevitably to the conclusion that the sufferer's family, and in particular, the mother, must be at fault! However, for the twenty-five years or so preceding the final confirmation that genetics play a significant part in schizophrenia, families were accused not just of being the missing environmental link but of actually causing the illness. Since about the mid 1970s, this sort of attitude has been largely frowned upon officially by the medical profession, but there are still health professionals, including some doctors, who have such views. As these sort of theories have had a profound effect on all involved with the illness, a more detailed discussion is probably worth while.

Back in the 1920s and 1930s, psychoanalysts were claiming that their skills and training enabled them to recognise schizophrenia as the result of traumatic early childhood experiences, no longer remembered or acknowledged. It is particularly interesting that the father of psycho-analysis, Freud, warned that psychosis would probably turn out to be of physical origin; he declined to work with schizophrenia eventually. However, the type of experience to which analysts referred is that which is likely to result from an unsatisfactory relationship with a cold, rejecting mother. In 1948, Fromm-Reichmann took this idea one step further by inventing a new phrase, the 'schizophrenogenic mother'[11] ('schizo-phrenogenic' means causing schizophrenia). Depending on the school of thought, mothers were variously described as cold, hostile, domineering, over-protective or over-involved. There were as many rationalisations for the frequent phenomenon of these same mothers having other offspring who were apparently normal.

These ranged from the position of the sick child in the family – eldest, middle, youngest – to the birthweight, or events in the mother's life around the time of that child's birth. In fact, you name it, and it has been suggested; and, of course, it is usually impossible to disprove theories of this type. It seems that psychoanalysts reason that faulty mothering affects the infant's developing 'ego' and that later – much later – this disintegrates under the stress of adolescence or early adulthood, causing severe regression back to infancy. The use of the word 'regression' to describe what happens to the individual in schizophrenia seems as strange as phrases like 'a happy release' to some of those who have close contact with the stoic courage and determination of many sufferers.

In 1956, Bateson and Jackson in the United States introduced a phrase that was to become common jargon in psychiatry; the 'double bind' communication.[12] This they defined as a message with a double meaning, commonly used, they believed, by relatives to those members of the family who later become schizophrenic. This theory emanated from their observation of families of newly diagnosed patients. They carefully made a note of every instance of such communication during their interviews with these families. (The reader may like to refer at this stage to comments on the likely behaviour of the patient prior to diagnosis, in Chapters 2 and 7.) Similar studies have been done on the families of anorexic patients, when the young person is hovering near to death from starvation. Thus, professionals observe other human beings in a state of crisis and yet find it significant when they record abnormal behaviour. The puzzling thing is that such studies are not seen as invaluable research on human behaviour in times of disaster. They are instead seen as valid recordings of the typical behaviour of such a family!

In the mid 1960s, Wynne and Singer started a series of studies on communication within families with a schizophrenic member.[13, 14] They seem persuaded that there is a subtle abnormality in communication between the parents, and from the parents to the child, that contributes to the development of the illness. However, other researchers have not been able to replicate their findings; Liem, for example, found that the parents' communication problems were more likely to be in response to abnormal messages from the sick child.[15]

Before concluding this discussion on distorted communication, and double-bind type messages, etc, I would like to divert for a moment to quote the late John Pringle, OBE, founder and former President of the National Schizophrenia Fellowship. In an article published in *The Times* on 9 May 1970, he commented that 'Failures in co-ordination and communication seem to hang about the administrative management of schizophrenia almost like a grim parody of the condition itself'.[16] I suspect this echoes the feelings of many of the families who have ever sought help for their schizophrenic relative. While the professionals have been studying families, the latter have had ample and frustrating opportunity to study the professionals' handling of this illness! It has been my interesting observation that schizophrenia provokes abnormal communication and, yes, double-bind messages, from all those involved with it, and by no means least from those concerned with the patient's treatment. This will be discussed further in the next chapter, as it seems to warrant careful consideration.

Following a responsible and detailed discussion of the above studies and many more of the same ilk, authors Neale and Oltmans comment that 'the double-bind concept has proved to be too elusive to measure reliably, and the notions associated with cold, domineering mothers and parental role reversals have not been confirmed'. They go on to say that 'several recent studies suggest that the parents' difficulties may be a response to the stress of living with a seriously disturbed child'.[17]

Nothing startling there, so why did the psychoanalytical lobby remain so powerful a force for so long a period in the treatment of this illness? Let us consider for a moment the phenomenon of the professional approach to schizophrenia; a very serious disease, it stands apart from all others in that families have been blamed for the patient's illness. Although that particular viewpoint is now frowned on officially, one of the most popular current theories now blames some families for causing relapses in their seriously ill relatives (see Chapter 4 for a detailed discussion on 'high expressed emotion' families).

Perhaps the popularity of 'family theories' in schizophrenia, despite a significant absence of evidence to support them, may reflect people's need to believe that dreadful things like this illness can only happen to somebody else; ie, to *those* families? Another explanation of the continuing popularity of such theories may be the growing resistance to the 'medical model' in some circles. The medical model is seen as being too rigid, implying a specific cause for a specific disability, demanding specific treatment. By implication, the patient becomes the passive victim of the all-powerful doctor. This viewpoint reflects a long power struggle within the health professions, together with a growing recognition of the need for an educated public to participate in the treatment processes and to be responsible for its own health. This latter viewpoint echoes my own sentiments, but 'the flight from the medical model'[18] in psychiatry, as Hoffer puts it, did nothing at all to further these aims. Because schizophrenia can divorce its victims from reality, it is an illness that is particularly needful of treatment in line with the medical model; how can a patient take responsibility for overcoming an illness that he or she does not recognise? There is plenty of time for that *once* the condition has been diagnosed and given appropriate treatment. There is a very real danger that with no requirement to provide a diagnosis, there is no need to provide treatment either! It was not unknown during the period we are discussing for a patient to be dismissed, albeit kindly, whilst all sorts of labels were pinned on his or her carers, usually starting with their sick need to scapegoat a family member and present the victim for treatment!

One other explanation for the seductiveness of family theories may be the innate implication that there is room for effective treatment with relationships within the family. Such a concept provides an attractive alternative to professionals who may otherwise feel impotent in the face of such a devastating disease; it certainly helps morale to feel that successful work can be attempted with a 'sick family'. However, the evidence does not support such ideas despite an inordinate amount of enthusiasm for them!

Fortunately, the advent of neuroleptic drug treatment in the early 1950s helped to restore the balance with its dramatic ability to alleviate the more florid symptoms of the illness for so many sufferers. This was discovered by accident as a result of a French surgeon experimenting with the use of antihistamine compounds for the purpose of preventing surgical shock. He noted that these produced alertness, but 'disinterest' in his patients. Doctors struggling with the treatment of mental illness were immediately interested in this discovery and by 1952 chlorpromazine and similar drugs were being used for the control of schizophrenia, for which they seemed to have a startlingly specific effect. Later, research was carried out to try to determine what it was in these various compounds that relieved many of the 'positive-type' symptoms. It was soon realised that they all act as dopamine receptor-blockers; it seems that the brain cells of schizophrenic patients either produce too much of this substance called dopamine, or they are unable to dispense with it in the usual manner. The neuroleptic drugs increase the turnover rate so that there is less 'spare' dopamine around.

The discovery of the significance of this particular neurotransmitter led to high hopes that the key had been found at last to the cause of schizophrenia. Sadly, this has not turned out to be the case. Although the important part played by dopamine is still the dominant theory, it is clear that this is by no means the whole story, even with those patients whose symptoms are dramatically relieved by the neuroleptic drugs. For example, some of the successful anti-psychotic medications concentrate less on dopamine and more on other neurotransmitters, with equally effective results.

At about the same time as the neuroleptic drugs came into use, Hoffer and Osmond, in Canada, were experimenting with the use of mega-vitamin treatment. In particular, they were interested in a transmethyl-ation hypothesis; they believed in the presence of an endogenous hallucinogen produced by an error in the individual's metabolism. Their theory was that large amounts of vitamin B_3 would correct this by absorbing excess methyl in the body, so they prescribed megavitamin doses of niacin or nicotinic acid, and sometimes vitamin C as well, to their patients. Although their work has not been substantiated by other researchers, patients and their families have been loud in their praises of the treatment received. It is often useful to ask the consumer about the product!

At the Brain Bio Centre in Princeton, USA, Pfeiffer and colleagues[19] feel that zinc and copper levels are often imbalanced and they are particularly interested in the blood histamine levels of schizophrenic patients. These sorts of measurements are used by these workers as part of a diagnostic yardstick for the treatment of sub-groupings of schizophrenic patients. They find a small proportion of sufferers are in fact exhibiting symptoms of severe food intolerance, so they always check for this before attempting to find any other cause of the illness.

Other theories have included a possible defect in carbohydrate mechanism and the belief that the typical 'low-drive' symptoms of the chronic form of the illness may be due to this. Frohman and colleagues found, in the early 1960s, that serum from approximately 60 per cent of chronic schizophrenics contained a protein factor that altered metabol-ism in chickens' red cells.[20] Later, Bergen and colleagues found plasma which, when injected into trained rats, adversely affected their rope-climbing abilities. Cells penetrated by this plasma had an increased uptake of various substances, all of which could apparently cause metabolic abnormalities.[21]

The last three examples of work carried out bring us back to our previous discussion about a missing environmental factor which influences the outcome of a genetically determined disease. It may be that we have an appropriate parallel in phenylketonuria, which is a serious disorder which can only be controlled by specific dietary management; this condition results from an enzyme deficiency. In this respect it is interesting to note that previous generations seem to have been much more aware of the importance of diet. The ancient Chinese proverb states 'Disease enters through the mouth', and remember the old saying 'One man's meat is another man's poison.' Coeliac disease caused havoc with its victims until the discovery was made that sufferers cannot tolerate gluten, which is a protein substance found in wheat, rye, barley and oats.

Two lots of researchers – Bender in 1953[22] and Graff and Handford in 1961[23] – have found a small, but significant, number of schizophrenic patients showing signs of coeliac disease, or with relatives who are coeliac. Dohan became interested in this idea, particularly when he noted that first-time admissions for schizophrenia decreased significantly in areas of Europe which experienced real grain shortages during World War II. He also noted that cultures which use maize and millet, in place of grains containing more gluten, have a lower incidence of the illness. In 1969,[24] and again in 1973 with Grasberger,[25] Dohan conducted experiments with a grain-free, milk-free diet and found this resulted in earlier discharge for hospitalised patients. Reintroduction of wheat gluten cancelled out this effect. Singh and Kay carried out similar work in 1976 which replicated these results.[26] Due to continuing anecdotal reports of dramatic effects for some sufferers who follow this sort of diet, attention has recently focused again on this subject. Various pieces of research have failed to replicate the findings of these earlier workers, but an interesting paper published in 1985[27] argues that these later studies have set out to prove something which has never been claimed; that sensitivity to gluten applies *across the board* for people with this illness. Similarly, samples would seem to have been too small to identify a factor which may well apply to a minority group of the total population with this diagnosis.

Whilst on the subject of the potentially adverse effects of one's lifestyle on some individuals, there is increasing evidence that the abuse of illegal drugs such as cannabis and LSD can lead into a schizophrenic illness. We do not know if this happens just to individuals who have a predisposition anyway to develop such an illness, nor whether it is the deciding factor or merely a trigger factor in such cases. What is certain is that there is a significant incidence of such drug-taking in the recent history of newly diagnosed cases and that where these sufferers continue to abuse these drugs then the prognosis is very poor.

During 1988 there was exciting news that a gene had been found that might be specific for schizophrenia.[28] Unfortunately, several other teams have not been able to replicate this work. Perhaps this is to be expected if schizophrenia does in fact represent a classic cluster of symptoms which nevertheless have more than one origin. Anyway, there is a great deal of work being carried out at the present time in this seemingly promising area of research.

Another avenue which might turn out to be equally important is the growing body of evidence pointing to the significance of possible brain trauma around the time of birth. It has been known for a long time that brain damage can lead to a psychosis with all the features of schizophrenia. Long-term studies[29,30,31] reveal a significant incidence of complications around the time of birth of those who later become schizophrenic. There is also interesting work[32] suggesting that where one of a pair of identical twins develops the illness, he or she is more likely to have a history of such complications than the twin who avoids this diagnosis.

There is no doubt that there is some exciting research being carried out with the help of modern technology techniques, despite a conspicuous lack of ready funding for this unfashionable cause. What sort of help is available, meanwhile, for those individuals who have already fallen victim to the illness?

4 Treatment under the NHS

Before the advent of neuroleptic drug treatment in the 1950s, doctors had precious few tools with which to relieve the symptoms of schizophrenia; only those patients who recovered spontaneously had much hope of leaving hospital to resume a normal life in the community. Apart from psychotherapy, which was available for a tiny minority of patients, there were three main types of treatment available: insulin coma, psycho-surgery, and electroconvulsive therapy.

INSULIN COMA

Since the 1920s, insulin had been given to psychiatric patients because of its sedative effect and its beneficial influence on appetite. It was noticed that schizophrenic patients who accidentally received enough insulin to go into a hypoglycaemic coma often seemed to come out of this with a lessening of their symptoms. Accordingly, it became a part of the treatment of some schizophrenic patients to be injected with doses of insulin until their blood sugar level dropped to a point where they became unconscious. The patient was then 'brought round' with glucose and this treatment was administered regularly over periods of perhaps two to three months. This did help a few patients. However, there was much conflicting evidence and some disillusionment with this time-consuming treatment.

PSYCHO-SURGERY

In 1935, some doctors started using psycho-surgery on their psychiatric patients and, in particular, they used the prefrontal lobotomy. This operation involved the destruction of nerve fibres on each side of the brain and did seem to help some very agitated, depressed patients. It was never shown to help schizophrenic patients in any way and yet the operation was performed on many such patients. As it was known to have

S-C

serious side-effects in that it could dramatically change personalities it was a worrying example of possible abuse of the individual's rights.

ELECTROCONVULSIVE THERAPY

Electroconvulsive therapy (ECT) became available in the late 1930s. In this treatment, a brief electric current is passed through the patient's brain. This is more often used for profound depressive states and, despite much propaganda to the contrary, it can dramatically relieve the misery of some patients. However, once again, ECT has not been found to be specifically helpful in schizophrenia and it therefore tends to be used only where depression is the dominant feature of the patient's illness, and where all else fails.

NEUROLEPTIC DRUG TREATMENT

In the early 1950s various drugs, based on antihistamine compounds, were found to be specifically helpful in the treatment of schizophrenia. (A more detailed discussion on the discovery of the power of these drugs will be found in Chapter 3.) In particular, they were found to have a dramatic effect on the 'positive-type' symptoms of schizophrenia. They are known as neuroleptic drugs. Green and Costain explain: 'Neuroleptic translated literally means acting on nerves and is used to mean drugs with therapeutic efficacy in the major psychotic or overactive psychiatric illnesses.'[1] Many such drugs have been marketed since the discovery of their value in the treatment of schizophrenia. Most can be given orally and some can be given by 'depot' injection, intramuscularly, usually via the buttocks. In this case, the drug is dissolved in an oily base and is released gradually into the system, providing longer-term, and better-controlled, distribution than that achieved with oral medication. It seems probable that the drug is better absorbed by this method. Depot injection has the additional advantage of ensuring that the medication is administered; patients are notoriously forgetful about taking oral medication. The nurse or doctor has a note of the date on which the next injection is due and can 'chase up' the patient if this is overlooked.

What do these drugs do? This was a question that occupied the minds of research workers in this field when they observed the marked effectiveness of this medication on schizophrenic symptoms. The first clue came in the early 1960s when it was realised that these drugs are dopamine antagonists. Dopamine is a neurotransmitter, a 'messenger', and it seems that there is too much of this substance in the brain cells of individuals with the positive-type symptoms of schizophrenia. The reader may like to refer back to Chapter 3 at this stage for a more detailed discussion on this subject, but it will suffice now to note that the main effect of the neuroleptic drugs seems to be the checking of this abundance of dopamine in the patient's brain cells. For a long time, this 'dopamine theory' seemed to be leading at last to the elusive cause of schizophrenia, but it is now realised that this is by no means the only factor in the potent effect of these drugs. Indeed, it may even prove to be of less importance than at first supposed; the activity of other neurotransmitters is also affected, for example, and little interest has yet been taken in the significance of the medication's antihistamine base.

In the first instance, it was the typical side-effects produced by the drugs that led to suspicion about dopamine. Parkinson's disease is partly caused by low levels of dopamine and it was quickly noticed that some schizophrenic patients treated with the neuroleptic drugs initially developed Parkinsonian-type symptoms. These symptoms include a pronounced tremor, shuffling gait, rigidity and drooling. Other similar side-effects, known as akathisia, produce a fidgeting restlessness, with constant pacing back and forth, and perhaps facial, finger and leg movements. There may also be dystonia- and dyskinesia-type twisting of the head, neck and body. At worst, symptoms may be quite dramatic with 'lock-jaw' and rolling back of the eyes. It must be emphasised quickly that all of these respond to anti-Parkinsonian drugs, such as benzhexol (Artane), orphenadrine (Disipal) and procyclidine (Kemadrin). At one time these were automatically prescribed with the neuroleptic drugs to avoid any side-effects. This is no longer the case and it is more usual to await the appearance of any symptoms before administering this sort of medication. Anti-Parkinsonian drugs should ideally only be prescribed if found to be necessary and just for as long as unwanted symptoms persist. The reason for this is that they may be implicated in the development of 'tardive dyskinesia', a more serious, belated and less frequent side-effect of taking neuroleptic drugs, with elderly patients seeming to be particularly at risk. This is a distressing condition, with involuntary movements of the face and tongue in particular, and it may be resistant to treatment, other than an increase in the neuroleptic medication already being administered. Ironically, until a harmless antidote for the florid symptoms of schizophrenia is found, there seems to be little choice but to accept the risks involved rather than allow the patient to suffer the miseries of unrelieved active psychosis. Meanwhile, research continues to formulate a drug which will obviate these unwelcome hazards.

Which are the drugs that so dramatically control or eliminate the positive-type symptoms of schizophrenia? The phenothiazine compounds are the major group of these neuroleptic drugs. These include chlorpromazine (Largactil), and fluphenazine, given as tablets (Moditen), and as depot injections (Modecate). Trifluoperazine is made up in tablets (Stelazine) and is rather less sedative than the others in this group. Thioridazine in tablet form (Melleril) is often the medication of choice for the elderly as it carries less risk of the extrapyramidal effects, discussed above, which are often more serious in this age group.

The thioxanthenes are another popular group of neuroleptic drugs, and these are flupenthixol (Depixol) and clopenthixol (Clopixol), both available as depot injections. These drugs are less sedating than the phenothiazines, and flupenthixol is not usually the drug of choice for over-excited patients.

The last major group are the butyrophenones, with haloperidol (Haldol or Serenace) being the most widely used and available both in tablets and as depot injections; it is longer lasting than the other depot injections. These drugs are more potent than the phenothiazines, but they can also produce more extrapyramidal side-effects. Derived from this group is an oral medication called pimozide (Orap) and this, too, has a longer-lasting effect than other oral neuroleptic drugs.

The choice of the drug naturally depends on the doctor supervising the patient and is also affected by the patient's particular requirements. Often the response of an individual to one of these drugs is not predictable and for that reason it may take a while to reach the stage where the medication is found which best controls the patient's symptoms without provoking unwanted side-effects.

Great passions are inflamed by the use of drug treatment in mental illness. Some critics believe that this amounts to an assault on the individual. They further believe that doctors are 'trigger-happy' when dealing out medication and intent on 'doping up' troublesome patients so that they will no longer create a nuisance. This sort of blanket condemnation may be a comfortable one for the conscience to adopt, but it fails to face up to the complex realities of mental illness. Doctors have a duty to relieve unnecessary suffering and to enable their patients to attain as good a state of health as is possible for them. It is an unfortunate dilemma for doctors generally that most drugs carry risks for some individuals. This applies in many fields of medicine, but it is in the field of psychiatry that most moral indignation is expressed. Presumably the basis for this sort of view is a continuing belief that a condition like schizophrenia is not really an *illness* at all.

Quite naturally, many doctors practising psychiatry are not keen to administer neuroleptic drugs unless they are convinced of the diagnosis and assured that the illness will return. Clearly, these drugs do present certain serious risks for some patients, but these have to be weighed against more immediate risks (such as those discussed in the case studies at the end of this chapter). It may be that these latter risks need to be emphasised more clearly. The British National Formulary (1985) states:

> Long term treatment of patients with a definite diagnosis of schizophrenia may be necessary even after their first episode of illness *in order to prevent the manifest illness from becoming chronic* [my italics]. Withdrawal of drug treatment requires careful surveillance because the patient who appears well on medication may suffer a disastrous relapse if treatment is withdrawn inappropriately. In addition, the need for continuation of treatment may not become immediately evident because relapse is often delayed for several weeks after cessation of treatment.[2]

It is common to meet families initially opposed to the idea of medication for their sick relative; it is rare to find any that continue to have this attitude after witnessing the dramatic relief of symptoms in the patient following such treatment. Many patients dislike taking medication, but not necessarily for the reasons we have been discussing. Their objections focus, naturally, on more mundane nuisance-value side-effects, such as the tendency to put on weight easily. Further, it is common for patients whose symptoms are not completely controlled by the medication to confuse continuing symptoms of the illness with side-effects of the drugs. It is noteworthy, therefore, that many patients do persevere with their medication. Many learn, from trial and error, that the more painful symptoms do return if they discontinue taking it. It is my belief that any patient who needs to take medication indefinitely, for any condition, deserves a careful explanation as to its function and its possible side-effects. As the schizophrenic patient becomes more aware of the medication's effects on his or her distressing symptoms, then professionals should be prepared to discuss the pros and cons of the drug and to listen to the patient's feelings and ideas about its effects. This way, the sufferer feels more in control of the situation and can learn to protect him- or herself by varying the dose according to the progress of the illness. This, of course, demands co-operation and flexibility from the doctors and nurses involved in ongoing supervision. Many patients benefit from this and develop insight into their own vulnerability.

A rather different issue is whether the administering of neuroleptic drugs is justified for the chronic sufferer who appears to obtain no relief of negative-type symptoms from them. This is a difficult matter to determine, as many such patients do suffer from the positive-type symptoms as well, albeit only intermittently, and there is a risk of 'acute' relapses. There is little doubt, however, that the medication does not have much effect on the chronic form of the illness.

As for the acute form of the illness, the majority of sufferers become, with the help of neuroleptic medication, well enough to live out in the community for most of the time. However, it is important to note that discharge from hospital does not in any way give an indication of quality of life. Many patients come out of hospital with their florid symptoms more or less under control, but by no stretch of imagination are they well, in the sense of being equipped to lead a normal life. It is my belief that this sometimes enormous gap between the results of neuroleptic drug treatment and the acquiring of good health *can* be bridged for many more sufferers; the second and third parts of this book deal with this subject. Meanwhile, we will look at other forms of available therapy, most of them complementary to drug treatment.

PSYCHOTHERAPY

This form of treatment has been available for most of this century and the reader may like to refer back to Chapter 3 for a discussion on the work and theories of those practising psychotherapy with schizophrenic patients. Here it suffices to say that no results with this approach have been shown to compete in any way with those of neuroleptic drug treatment insofar as the alleviation of the symptoms of schizophrenia is concerned.

A word of caution: the psychoanalytic and interpretative approach can be dangerous for schizophrenic patients. Most authorities now agree that it is unwise to 'probe' in this illness and, indeed, families have been accused of damaging sufferers this way. One obvious example of the danger of an intense 'one-to-one' therapy situation is that patients often suffer from excessive guilt feelings and can torture themselves with misgivings after confiding what may well be quite insignificant items of information to the therapist.

Another form of psychotherapy, one that is entirely supportive and enabling, can be very helpful. It is to be hoped that this approach may become more widely used. It should focus on encouraging the patient to discuss any lingering symptoms freely with the therapist, either individually or within a group, so that the opportunity is provided for discussion of the quirks of the illness, rather than quirks in the patient! This enables patients to understand that they are suffering from common symptoms and so to learn better how to live with them. Patients should be encouraged to talk about the problems and setbacks of everyday life, in the light of their illness, with discussion of ways to tackle these. This approach is particularly useful in a group-work setting and the reader may care to refer to Chapter 8 for a more detailed discussion of this approach, apparently rare at the present time.

BEHAVIOUR MODIFICATION

This approach has become popular recently. It has the attraction that it enables ward staff to be involved in an active treatment programme. The idea is that certain forms of behaviour in the patient are identified as undesirable and socially unacceptable. Patient and staff then enter into a contract by which the elimination of such behaviour is rewarded. When this approach is limited to the use of 'social skills' programmes or group-work, it can be very constructive. Behaviour that will cause the patient embarrassment or hostility out in the community becomes the focal point and behaviour-modification techniques can be a useful tool in rehabilitation programmes. 'Social skills' groups can be used to encourage certain behaviours or skills lost during the patient's illness, as well as discouraging negative behaviour.

However, when a general behavioural approach is adopted on the ward or in the day hospital, for example, there are inherent dangers. The patient tends to be seen in a 'deviant' role rather than in the rightful 'sick' role, with the dignity and self-respect that this implies. Staff may come to see behaviour provoked by a serious illness as 'bad' behaviour. They mistakenly judge the actions of a sick patient on their understanding of their *own* behaviour. This is quite inappropriate and leads to the frequent use of emotive phrases such as 'manipulative' behaviour and 'attention-seeking' behaviour. Falling asleep in a group, for example, can be described as the latter! Staff who are skilled in other ways become judges and lay-psychologists, and patients lose what little remains of their self-respect together with their respect for the staff; judgemental attitudes reveal little real understanding of the illness and a 'them and us' situation can prevail.

Fortunately, these pitfalls are usually avoided, but it is very important that staff should be aware of them. Mentally ill patients are very sensitive and they are adults; a general behavioural approach can tend to overlook both these points. The patient will not learn to accept himself or herself, failings and all, unless he or she feels respected by staff and other patients alike.

FAMILY THERAPY

In the days when credence was given to theories that the schizophrenic patient was the well member of a sick family, work was done attempting to alter relationships and communication within families. In retrospect, Neale and Oltmanns report that:

> ... the promise of family treatment methods has not been rigorously tested ... it is not clear that existing methods of treatment that focus on these relationships are able to effect a positive change in the schizophrenic's adjustment.[3]

Meanwhile, some researchers firmly believe that the family's reaction to the patient's illness can influence the rate of relapse. Following earlier studies,[4,5] in 1972 Brown and colleagues studied families of schizophrenic patients in the home immediately following the breakdown and hospitalisation of the sufferer. They measured levels of 'expressed emotion', which was judged by the level of critical comment (bearing in mind the content and the tone of the voice), hostility or emotional over-involvement. They found that patients returning to families with high expressed emotion were more likely to relapse than others. In 1976, Vaughn and Leff[6] replicated these findings; 58 per cent of the patients in high-expressed-emotion families suffered a relapse, and only 16 per cent of those in low-expressed-emotion families did so. As a result of these two studies, the term 'high expressed emotion' ('high EE') has become as much part of medical jargon as the phrase 'double bind' was throughout the 1970s.

It seems that the motivation for this type of research was prompted by the frequent relapses suffered by some chronically ill patients. As Green and Costain point out: 'Recurrent acute episodes or relapse of illness are common, sometimes apparently precipitated by failure to take medication, but often for some unknown reason.'[7] It is perhaps natural that the medical profession look for a reason in the community when a 'revolving door' patient returns to hospital for treatment. Nevertheless it seems to be overlooked that long-term hospitalised patients also suffer relapse; ward staff refer to the patient going through a 'bad phase' with bouts of depression or unexplained violence. Such swings are promptly treated by adjustment of medication and the patient comes out of the bad phase or whatever with little damage having been done. It is not quite so easy out in the community! With the almost inevitable delay in obtaining treatment, the patient often deteriorates to the point where the family can no longer gain his or her co-operation to accept medication, or an adjustment of medication, and readmission to hospital becomes almost inevitable. This usually involves considerable trauma for both patient and family; the latter frequently feel pangs of guilt at the patient's distress and blame themselves for letting it all happen once again. It was at such times that the interviews measuring levels of expressed emotion were carried out.

The danger with the sort of work described above is that it escalates such feelings. Don Young, Director of the Schizophrenia Association of Great Britain, concludes, at the end of a responsible and carefully argued critique of this research: 'It seems that the whole responsibility for relapse with its attendant burden of guilt is being placed once again on the shoulders of the carers.'[8] This seems to be a valid statement in the face of years of what one can only describe as 'family bashing' by some professionals.

The danger with this particular work is that we probably have, once again, a 'chicken and egg' situation. If we were not so occupied looking for aggravation of this illness within the family, we would surely be concerned about the damage that might be suffered by this same family in trying to cope with the devastation caused by schizophrenia. In doing so, we would note that the family were indeed 'uptight' ('high EE' in professional jargon) and we would suspect that this might be an indicator of the severity of symptoms in the patient. Instead, we conclude that the family's 'uptight' attitude is a cause of the patient's relapse rather than an expression of the desperation felt by all concerned and, very probably, an indicator of the extent of the patient's handicap, in terms of coping with life in the community.

From this family's point of view, not only do we show little concern for their plight, but we have the temerity to blame them for relapses in the patient. We have just as little understanding of the remissions and relapses in another serious illness – multiple sclerosis – but, up to now, no one seems to blame the patient's carers for these.

There are, of course, several queries raised by this research – and I refer in particular to the 1976 study. For instance, relapsing patients tended to be those who had excessive 'face-to-face' contact with carers; we need to know if this was a direct result of the severity of their illness, as is so often the case – they cannot be 'contained' in any of the available day care resources. Also, patients in 'high EE' families tended to rely more on medication; as this is an essential factor in maintaining good health in sufferers who periodically have 'positive' symptoms, this would in itself indicate a likelihood of intermittent relapse. This is less common in the sufferer with 'negative' symptoms who, of course, usually obtains little relief from medication. In this context, I would remind the reader of

Richter's comment (already quoted in Chapter 1): 'the present position is that schizophrenia is currently recognised as a term applied to a group of similar, but by no means identical mental illnesses.'[9] One wonders how researchers satisfy themselves that they are in fact working with a sample of exactly similar cases by which they can attempt to judge these other variables.

'Over-involvement' was another measure used; it is the writer's experience that this is indeed an indicator of both a type of illness and the severity of the illness; it is usually most pronounced just prior to diagnosis (ie, where schizophrenia is evident, but untreated) and it fades with the patient's return to reasonable health.

One very interesting aspect of the research was the comparison of schizophrenic patients with depressive patients. The results of this aspect of the work are summed up in the authors' own words: 'The depressed patients in our sample are even more vulnerable to the effects of relatives' criticism than are the schizophrenics and have a tendency to relapse at a lower level of criticism.'[10] Why do we not hear about 'high EE' families in the treatment of depressive illness? It seems that this work confirms what we would all expect in any event; stress (in the form of loved ones' attitudes) is unproductive. However, this work also suggests that schizophrenic patients may have some sort of defence mechanism that makes them a lot less vulnerable to such stress *or* that their 'reading' of their relatives' attitudes is quite different to that of the 'experts', as the vital number of criticisms for depressive patients was *two* as against *six* for the schizophrenic patient! Finally, and to quote the researchers' own words, '42 per cent of the patients returning to high EE families *managed to stay well* [my italics].

As part of a large study just completed by researchers at Northwick Park Hospital, MacMillan and colleagues discuss this work and say that their own findings cast 'considerable doubt on recent speculations that important predictors of outcome are present in the family environment'.[14] It is significant that this is the first work of its kind attempted with families of first-time hospital admissions. Attitudes of relatives, therefore, were not unduly influenced by the 'wearing down' process of caring for a chronically ill sufferer over a long period with all the trauma caused by seemingly inevitable relapses. These researchers conclude 'the most important clinical implication of the findings . . . is to introduce a note of caution toward enthusiastic and generalised therapeutic interpretations of studies of the family environment in schizophrenia'.[15] The whole of the Northwick Park Study of First Episodes of Schizophrenia[16] is well worth reading as it details the sort of problems and delays families experience initially when trying to obtain help for a sick relative and it includes findings that point to the value of early diagnosis and treatment, and continuing drug therapy.

Much earlier, Prof Wing gave some indication of the tightrope facing the schizophrenia sufferer in the community:

> On the one hand, too much social stimulation, experienced by the patient as *social intrusiveness*, may lead to an acute relapse. On the other hand, too little stimulation will exacerbate any tendency already present towards social withdrawal, slowness, underactivity, and an apparent lack of motivation[11]

What skills patients and their families have to develop in the interests of survival!

Wing further comments:

> It is extraordinary that so many relatives do manage to find a way of living with schizophrenia that provides the patient with a supportive and non-threatening home. Some of the factors that are to some extent under their control are as follows:
>
> Creating a non-critical, accepting environment
> Providing the optimal degree of social stimulation
> Keeping aims realistic
> Learning how to respond to delusions and bizarre behaviour
> Making use of whatever social and medical help is available
> Learning to use welfare arrangements
> Obtaining rewards from the patient's presence
> Helping patient's attitudes to self, to relatives, to medication, to work

All of these aspects are covered in some detail in this book, mostly in Part II; they are the ingredients of survival for both the patient and the family. Perhaps it is possible that family-therapy techniques could be used to help fulfil some of these aims, *from the time of diagnosis*, but only if the therapists concerned are fully conversant with the problems experienced in living with schizophrenia.

Meanwhile, another worrying aspect of the sort of research discussed above is that it tends to provoke advice from well-meaning professionals to encourage patients to live away from the family home; all of the 'family theories' have rather naturally contributed to this sort of advice being handed out frequently. I believe this to be of such consequence that it deserves serious consideration at this point.

Firstly, it should be clear that seeking a return to good health and a normal way of life implies that the prior aim should be to encourage independence and self-sufficiency in the sufferer. Hopefully, this will eventually lead to separate living arrangements, whether the sufferer marries or not. Few adults want to live indefinitely in the parental home, but most appreciate frequent contact with the family once they have left home; it is rewarding to know that one 'belongs' and that there is no need to feel alone at bad times. This, then, is the ideal solution for the partly disabled sufferer or, for that matter, for the elderly widowed grandmother; independent living, with a warm welcome waiting in the family home. How practical is such an arrangement for the newly diagnosed schizophrenic patient, about to be discharged from hospital, for example? It is my belief that such a proposal for the patient who has previously lived as a member of the family home can be dangerous. Whether the suggestion comes from professionals or from the family itself, the patient may interpret it as rejection, and punitive rejection at that. Remember, the admission to hospital has very probably followed a long period of quite severe suffering for the patient, who may well have harboured paranoid feelings about the family as well. Most of us know the deep longing to return home as soon as possible if we have to go into hospital at any time; the confused sufferer is no different. I do not believe this is the time to separate the patient from his or her family, *unless* the patient or the family, or both, are adamant about not wanting to persevere with the arrangement. If that is the case, then there is important work to be covered by the professionals concerned so that relationships can be salvaged as far as is possible and to discourage needless feelings of guilt on either side.

One of the reasons commonly offered for recommending that the patient should live away from the family is the frequently found over-involvement between the patient and a member of the family, probably the mother. This is discussed in some detail in Chapter 8 and elsewhere in this book, but suffice it to say at this point that this is a sign of remaining impairment; the dependency will *not* be severed by forcibly separating the parties concerned. Relationships will normalise with returning good health, and, meanwhile, the patient is clearly demonstrating a need for this 'crutch'. It is far more productive to make sure that the family have advice on how to handle this sort of problem (and this is discussed further in Chapter 8) than to rely on 'separation' to solve it. I say 'separation' with some irony, because this will not in any event be achieved unless the patient's paranoia and feelings of rejection cause him or her to withdraw completely from the family. This should not be allowed to happen; no professionals can offer the amount of support that is needed to help the patient learn to survive with his or her new handicap. Few professionals have the time available to carry out more than one visit per week to their most vulnerable clients/patients. To give just one example of the problems to be overcome; whatever arrangements are made for the sufferer during the daytime, who is to get him or her out of bed in the morning (many find it nigh impossible to cope with this first priority in the day's routine)?

Perhaps it would be more profitable to suggest that the reader considers this discussion further after reading Chapters 7, 8 and 9; it may then be more clear why I have been convinced for many years that separation from the family should come later and, preferably, when the sufferer has learned to cope with his or her handicap, even if this is just a remaining vulnerability to further relapse.

As the next two chapters will illustrate, society has not come up with any alternatives to the family for the permanently impaired sufferer. There are cases where the severity of the illness makes life a nightmare for the family and it is clearly the responsibility of the State to provide a refuge for such patients. For these, and for those who cannot live with the family for whatever reason, it becomes harder and harder to find such refuge, so it would seem profoundly sensible and desirable to offer as much support as possible to all those families who are more fortunate and do feel able to cope.

It seems probable that family therapy techniques can be usefully employed in this direction, particularly if these focus on the sort of factors that Prof Wing pinpoints as 'to some extent [being] under their [relatives'] control'; this sort of work, of course, demands a very thorough understanding of the difficulties of coping with schizophrenia.

FAMILY GROUP-WORK

A cheaper and very effective way of achieving these aims can be by the use of group-work methods. It has long been realised that self-help groups are very effective in dealing with various problems. The National Schizophrenia Fellowship has probably achieved as much by these methods as has anything provided by the statutory services for schizophrenia sufferers. Group-work with relatives can follow the lines of the work done in local NSF groups. Professionals working in this way need only to provide relevant information about the illness and be there to answer any specific queries that are not answered by other relatives from their own experiences. This sort of work provides an invaluable learning experience, and is rewarding – and cost-effective as well.

Meanwhile, there are signs at the time of writing that before very long, families will at last be recognised as the 'primary carers' – see Appendices

II and III. When this happens, patient and relatives may be involved in treatment plans from the onset of the illness and will also benefit from sharing all the available information. It is my belief that this sort of family work will achieve more for the patient's well-being than all the work based on 'family theories' put together.

SUMMARY OF AVAILABLE TREATMENT

Under the National Health Service at the present time, the vast majority of schizophrenic patients receive neuroleptic drug treatment at some time. A few are also treated by ECT, and fewer still by individual psychotherapy. More often, group-work methods are used with patients in hospitals and other institutions and, increasingly, a behaviour-modification approach is found. Possible hazards in drug treatment, coupled with the stigma attached to the illness, make some doctors very reluctant to diagnose schizophrenia, and to treat accordingly. Earlier theories that families caused the illness are no longer officially credited, but continue to be very popular with some professionals.

HOW DOES ALL THIS WORK IN PRACTICE?

Ideally, when the family, or whoever, notices a worrying change in the personality of the sick individual there is a positive response from the GP, with referral to a specialist who can diagnose the illness. If the sufferer then receives medication and is fortunate enough to obtain immediate relief of the worst symptoms, then hospitalisation may not be necessary. In any event, it is quite common for a short stay in hospital to be all that is required and, as long as appropriate after-care is provided, the patient can learn how to cope with the illness at home. Hopefully, the family will by now have been given vital knowledge about schizophrenia and the sort of difficulties to expect. Sooner or later, the patient will need to share such knowledge; meanwhile, family and professionals will make sure that medication is taken regularly in order to avoid an unnecessary relapse.

Sadly, things do not often work out this way and it may be useful at this stage to pause and consider the sort of experiences that can cause so much avoidable despair to families trying to obtain help for a sick relative. Many health professionals I have worked with feel that it is wrong, almost immoral, to label an individual with the diagnosis of 'schizophrenia' – that is, until such time as the individual is clearly disabled beyond any question or doubt. However, from the patient's point of view, no diagnosis often means no effective treatment. Surely there can be little worse than suffering from this dreaded illness *and having this unrecognised by those who can provide a remedy*. It must be rather like screaming for help if you were being attacked by thugs, with passers-by deciding it would be imprudent to intervene.

There is, however, a subtle difference. The passer-by is there by chance; not so the professional who is trained and paid to be there specifically to alleviate the suffering of those referred for help. Health professionals may appreciate that some of our reluctance to diagnose schizophrenia lies in our own 'gut' feelings about this dreaded condition. Professionals shudder when it comes to informing a patient or the family of the diagnosis; in contrast, the patient and the family usually speak of feelings of profound relief and hope when they eventually learned of a diagnosis that explained the strange experiences and behaviour that had plagued their lives for so long.

Gwynneth Hemmings, founder of the Schizophrenia Association of Great Britain, comments:

> So often the schizophrenic patient is not given a diagnosis, is not told he has a real disease which has altered his normal brain and body chemistry and so, without the sick role, he is left in a terrifying vacuum . . . deprived of the all-essential information about his disease.[13]

Let us look at three brief case histories which illustrate what tends to happen when the diagnosis is withheld, or not recognised, in those important early days of the onset of the illness.

TOM: This young man made life so intolerable in his home, eventually blacking both his mother's eyes when she tried to get him up one morning, that in the end the parents gave up the struggle and turned him out of the home. This is a caring family, but their pleas for help were ignored and they were given no explanation for behaviour which was terrorising the two younger children in the household. Two admissions to hospital had produced no diagnosis and no guidance as to how to cope with this now unrecognisable son. No treatment was offered, other than family therapy sessions, which the sufferer did not bother to attend.

During the next two years, the parents had to keep finding new lodgings for Tom and help was only forthcoming when he was found trying to set fire to a boarding-house. This, it seemed, was an act which befitted a serious diagnosis and the label of schizophrenia! On medication, his health is steadily improving and the family are becoming reunited.

Tom had previously been a happy and sociable lad, with a bright future;

his life was nearly in ruins when help was finally provided. It possibly came only just in time to prevent an untimely death. Would any of the health professionals involved with this lad's 'treatment' have been able to cope any better than these parents and would they be satisfied with a similar approach to illness in *their* families?

SARAH: A bright, sensitive young woman, Sarah was allowed to deteriorate for a period of four years, despite her well-educated parents' pleas for help within months of her personality beginning to change. Eventually, they found her suicide note even as they were persuading a doctor to admit her to hospital. Several days later, Sarah ran into the road in front of passing traffic outside the hospital, where she was convinced the staff were trying to poison her.

She made a dramatic recovery on neuroleptic medication, and with the sort of measures described in Part II and Part III of this book, achieved a normal lifestyle several years later.

For nearly four years, the parents' pleas for help and the girl's evident misery were dismissed by professionals as 'over-protectiveness', 'personality disorder', etc. Once more, help arrived only just in time to prevent death by suicide or accident. It did not come in time to prevent a prolonged period of mental torture; Sarah's subsequent response to treatment demonstrates beyond any doubt that this was absolutely avoidable.

JOANNE: This lively, attractive young mother suffered a second breakdown (the first having been described as 'an adolescent disturbance'). When it was realised that Joanne was in fact mildly psychotic, neuroleptic medication was promptly administered. This revived her to her usual self. Not long afterwards, her family became concerned that she might become dependent on her 'tranquillisers' and persuaded Joanne to stop taking her tablets.

The family, like the patient herself, were unaware of the diagnosis. More seriously, they were unaware of her vulnerability and the need for her to take medication for at least the foreseeable future. Joanne relapsed badly several weeks later and this time she had to be admitted to hospital, with all the misery that this entailed for a mother of two very young children.

When I knew Joanne, she was desperately worried about her marriage. She felt thoroughly inadequate and blamed herself for her inability to cope, in the absence of a diagnosis that would have made her performance not only appropriate but, indeed, courageous. The doctor in charge of her supervision refused to permit colleagues to share with the young woman and her family the true diagnosis and advice on maintaining good health. I wonder if Joanne eventually obtained this information and I wonder if she managed to save the marriage that was so precious to her?

I believe these three – not untypical – examples illustrate at least one common phenomenon in the treatment of schizophrenia: our disastrous disregard for the testimony and the survival instinct of that vital institution, the family. It is within our own families that we demonstrate our qualities and our failings. We no longer play whatever roles are expected of us in our daily lives; we come home and we relax. It is our families who know us intimately, for better or for worse! It is our families who sense any change in us. As we discussed in Chapter 2, the onset of schizophrenia is often notoriously insidious; that is, it creeps up on the individual so slowly and imperceptibly that even the family may be deceived for a time. Outsiders certainly are, and for very much longer. Once the family is sure there is something very wrong, *they should be listened to.* We should not fall back on theories such as 'I wonder why this mother *needs* a sick child?' (I heard this question again recently; it use to be voiced frequently). What the mother *does* need is that the professionals should take her concern seriously. Once the diagnosis is made, it is still important that the professionals continue to listen to the family because it is the latter who will first notice any signs of relapse. For instance, let me quote the example of one family's efforts to obtain help.

JACKIE: This young woman, in her late twenties, suffers from auditory hallucinations most of the time. Despite her unusually severe symptoms, her mother and sister have managed to support Jackie in the community during the past two years. When she started to relapse, the mother begged for help and when Jackie was admitted to hospital one month later the mother had still not been granted an interview with the doctor who supervises this patient's treatment.

At the time of writing, Jackie has been back in hospital for two months and has lost 1½ stones in weight. The mother does not look much better herself. It may be interesting to note that this particular psychiatrist is one of those who firmly believe that families are the cause of relapse in patients . . .

What is it about this illness that overrides people's basic common sense (and I am not referring to its victims!). Common sense should be our strongest weapon in the fight against schizophrenia and this would involve us in direct, straightforward action. Instead, distorted communication is the rule rather than the exception. Attitudes towards the illness influence the timing of the diagnosis, the likelihood of such a diagnosis being made, the acknowledgement or otherwise of this diagnosis, and whether or not the patient and family will receive an explanation of what is happening to them. I was told by a psychiatrist, not very long ago, that schizophrenia was far too serious an illness for the patient to be burdened with the diagnosis. He went on to explain that recent 'literature' on the subject recommends that the sufferer just be left to 'get on with life' and this is possible so long as he or she is not labelled!

This was an interesting example of 'double bind' communication. From the patient's point of view, he or she then has no diagnosis, no sick role and no explanation for what is happening; I find this indefensible in itself, but just let the patient attempt to obtain a pensionable job, or to emigrate, for example, and this non-existent diagnosis will almost certainly militate against such plans. Once again, the patient is left facing a reality that others are avoiding!

IGNORANCE, FEAR AND STIGMA

These seem to be the themes underlying so much of the handling of this illness. If we could overcome these connotations and treat schizophrenia as the disease it is, I believe we could start to win the battle. The reality, whether we like it or not, is that *at least* one in every hundred of us is at risk and in need of urgent help (I personally believe it is more than one in every hundred). For some, the battle may already be lost if help is not provided in the early stages of the illness and for others it may still be lost if the individual is not made fully aware of the dangers that remain. In both instances, this is, in my view, an avoidable tragedy in terms of human waste, unfulfilled promise, and a diminished quality of life. Surely this should fill us with more dread than the stigma of a diagnosis that won't be stifled indefinitely in any event? Those patients whose treatment avoids this sort of pitfall have reason indeed to be grateful and many are able to resume normal lives despite having contracted schizophrenia.

In the next chapter, we shall take a look at the concept of 'community care', which assumes increasing importance as doctors have fewer and fewer hospital beds available to them for their patients.

5 Resources in the Community

At the time of writing it seems almost inevitable that the remaining mental hospitals will be shut down in the next few years, despite the growing misgivings of many of those who originally supported the closure programme. What alternatives do we have for disappearing hospital beds? Five years ago a National Schizophrenia Fellowship publication commented:

> The services and other help actually provided for people with chronic mental disorders display large gaps and serious inadequacies. In contrast with a romantic vision of help from informal community networks, people discharged from hospital are often socially isolated and unoccupied, sometimes in poverty if not destitution. They and their relatives, if any, are given little guidance on how to 'live with mental illness'. Out-patient clinics are crowded; getting help in an emergency is often difficult; and the social services give psychiatric disorders a very low priority. Residential and day care units are scarce and understaffed. Co-ordination between services is usually poor.[1]

It is unlikely that anyone at all familiar with the situation would argue with this appraisal. What are the resources which may be available to sufferers within the community? These may be divided into four main groups; human, housing, day-care and welfare benefits. Let's look first at the human resources:

Families

Many relatives claim that they provide the only community care at the present time, a claim that may well be justified. Depending on the extent of the handicap of each particular sufferer, care from the family will range from the extra interest and support required when someone you love can be at risk of further breakdown at any time, through to a constant vigil in which the carer has no respite for socialising, for hobbies, for holidays or, perhaps, even for private space and moments of peace; all of the things that most of us take for granted. On top of this, many have to contend with continual financial hardship generated from problems and needs created by a chronic illness, and in particular a schizophrenic illness. The 'family' is in fact all too frequently a woman, a mother, otherwise isolated as the rest of her relatives give up the struggle and leave her to soldier on alone. Sadly, it is not uncommon for any professionals concerned to do this too. Two social workers quote an example of the sort of predicament in which some carers find themselves:

'Well he's home now and they told me on the ward that he's schizophrenic. I'm not sure what that means but I do know that for my son it's like being in a cage that's made of glass but the thing is society seems to have locked us in there, too. We can see the people outside, I'm shouting for help and they pass by, social workers, doctors, nurses. I can't make them hear what it's like for me or get them to unlock the door with their knowledge and understanding . . . I want to help him but I need to know how . . . Can you let me know where to go from here and call in to see me sometime? My family won't come any more.'[2]

General Practitioners
It is a sad fact that most of these doctors have received little training in psychiatry and even less in recognising the warning signs of a developing schizophrenic illness. In 1988, a junior Health Minister, when stressing the importance of 'prevention' in mental illness, mentioned the possibility of 'finding ways of helping GPs identify and treat psychiatric problems at an early stage'[3]. The need for such measures is borne out by a finding of a survey carried out within the membership of the National Schizophrenia Fellowship that in 185 out of 889 first episodes of the illness, the doctor was not prepared to treat the problem seriously.[4] GPs are the gateway to all the mental health services, yet in 1981 the Acheson Report[5] pointed out that in addition to little or no specific training in dealing with mental illness being available to them, there was also a lack of awareness in the profession of other relevant services and resources. Unless such problems are addressed, there seems little likelihood of much preventative work being achieved with this illness. Where the GP is aware of the warning signs of a first breakdown or relapse in schizophrenia, and where the practice liaises with all the local mental health services, then sufferers and families tend to fare very much better than when this is not the case.

Psychiatrists
Despite the talk for several decades of community care, there is little evidence as yet of these specialists being any more available to sufferers

and carers in the community. A recent NSF and SANE publication suggests that psychiatrists need to spend as much time with relatives as with their patients, preferably seeing both in their homes, and points out that 'the experience many psychiatrists have of schizophrenia has been within a hospital, not the hurly burly of life'.[6] Of course, some psychiatrists are trying to find ways of working more meaningfully within the community, but one of the factors militating against this is the pressure of numbers on their caseloads. In a situation where even emergency domiciliary visits to assess the need for compulsory admission to hospital can be delayed several days – sometimes more – the hope that these specialists might routinely visit families in their homes seems to be ambitious, to say the least.

One of the main frustrations of the out-patient system which is regularly voiced by sufferers who are given appointments on a three-monthly or six-monthly basis is that they rarely see the same doctor more than once or twice, so this potentially valuable consultation consists of a few routine questions from a stranger who has no time to get to know the patients nor to gain their trust. The current method of training junior doctors seems to be as much at fault here as does the pressure of time on their seniors. It seems that it is assumed that meeting a variety of patients on a 'one-off' basis is an essential component of training.

For all sorts of reasons, then, psychiatrists remain elusive to sufferers in the community and even more so to their families. Some of these doctors partly resolve this dilemma by keeping closely in touch with colleagues of other disciplines who may be working with their patients in the community so that they can intervene at any reported sign of threatened relapse. This is an excellent way of spreading their services more widely and sufferers are usually content to know that the supervising doctor is still interested and kept aware of their progress.

Clinical Psychologists
In many areas these professionals are not involved with individuals suffering from psychotic illnesses such as schizophrenia. They tend to work with neurotic patients and any others whose problems are not usually responsive to drug treatment. Having said that, there are notable exceptions and some psychologists are in the front line of the battle against schizophrenia, both by working with sufferers and families and by carrying out valuable research into positive ways of coping with the illness.[7]

Social Workers

Those who are based in psychiatric hospitals tend to have some experience of working with families trying to cope with this illness and a few have chosen to specialise and build up an expertise in the field. Most, however, do not practise in the community and their colleagues who do so have had little opportunity over the past two decades to work with mental illness. In the early 1970s specialisation in social work departments went out of fashion and the much respected and valued mental welfare officers disappeared with it. For this reason and because social work departments have been increasingly weighed down with statutory responsibilities for children, the mentally ill have become a very low priority on social workers' caseloads. However, the Mental Health Act, 1983, gives those officers who work with the legislation – ie approved social workers (ASWs) – special and new responsibilities and requires them to undergo extra training in mental health law and in working with the mentally ill. Hopefully, this, and an increasing tendency for social service departments to return to specialisation, will eventually lead to opportunities for interested social workers to work more with the mentally ill and to develop a real expertise again. Meanwhile, after the first few years of ASW training programmes, the social workers themselves report that they do not feel they are learning enough about the 'mentally ill and matters directly relevant to the mentally ill'.[8] Families trying to cope with schizophrenia tend very much to agree that this is the case and it would seem that neither the social worker nor the client is having a fair deal at the present time.

Community Psychiatric Nurses

The role of the community psychiatric nurse (CPN) is a supporting and monitoring one. Initially, the work was confined to those patients discharged from the mental hospital to which the nurse was attached. More recently, it is becoming common for CPNs to take referrals from GPs and, in some cases, to be attached to a health centre or to a multi-GP practice. This is one of several factors leading to the service playing an increasingly active role in assessment and preventative work and, in doing so, also working with a new client population of what is sometimes called 'the worried well'. This is creating a situation where more and more CPNs can be employed and yet the needs of the chronically ill still be overlooked. At the end of the 1980s, a few area health authorities still employ no CPNs at all, while there are others which are content to allow their nurses to work on an 'open-referral' system in which they choose the cases with whom they wish to work! As many professionals find monitoring and supporting schizophrenia sufferers on a long-term basis both demanding and unrewarding, such an approach can result in this particularly vulnerable population having minimal support from a service that originated to meet its needs out in the community; a situation, in fact, where the more seriously ill are not catered for. Towards the end of the 1980s, a junior Health Minister commented in the House of Commons that this phenomenon is widespread and occurring in other countries as well as here:

> Professionals working with mentally ill people tend to concentrate on mild illness, as opposed to severe illness, as more people move from institutions into the community.[9]

In those areas where such important matters have received adequate consideration, the CPN is proving to be the ideal link between medical supervision and independent life in the community for many sufferers who need continuing care. Where such a service is offered, it is significant that it is usually much appreciated both by sufferers and by carers, and it is only marred where too-heavy caseloads result in less and less available time for this very needy population as well as 'burn out' and sickness in exhausted practitioners.

Occupational Therapists
Increasingly, these previously hospital-based professionals will move out into the community and should have much to offer, particularly in terms of assisting some sufferers to 'set up house' on their own and others to structure their time more rewardingly.

HOUSING AND OTHER ACCOMMODATION___

What sort of accommodation is available to those sufferers for whom living with their families is not an option? As some of the hospitals are closing down, some of the most seriously ill long-term patients are being transferred to other hospitals or moved out into hostels that resemble hospital wards, but without the variety of services and facilities available in the old institutions. Another type of hospital service moving out into the community is the hospital rehabilitation hostel, which again is usually staffed by qualified nurses and is of a very high material standard. Again, this is an expensive option and a rare one, and the facility will become blocked unless there is pressure maintained to move residents on. But to move on to where? Very few areas have planned to provide a series of housing resources that allow for gradual progression from well-supported housing through to more independent living[10] – and where they have, this is rarely on a scale that will meet the growing need for sheltered housing.

Increasingly, voluntary organisations, housing associations and private enterprises are providing various types of hostel accommodation. Some are staffed by individuals with expertise in working with mental illness; others are not. Some use a 'medical model' approach, acknowledging the importance of drug treatment and alertness to early signs of relapse; some do not. Some expect their residents to take responsibility for their own health and lifestyle, with dire results for some of those who have a schizophrenic illness.

For several decades, group homes have proved to be a cheap and effective method of providing sheltered housing for the chronically ill in the community. Any number from two to six or so individuals can be housed together, ideally having separate bedrooms and communal dining, cooking and bathroom facilities. The usual choice of accommodation is ordinary local housing so that something approaching real integration into the neighbourhood is achieved. The success of this approach depends to a large extent on the amount of preparation provided for the residents in the art of group-living and in the appropriate skills required to cope with everyday life in the community. Even more important is continuing support and supervision, with ideally a social worker or CPN involved in at least once-weekly visits, and also some suitable voluntary support. It is also important that residents should be encouraged to go out several times in the week to take part in some sort of activity. Where such standards are not achieved, then there is a tendency for group homes to become little more than 'mini institutions' of the less desirable kind.

Another type of sheltered housing, which can encourage independent living even where families are still supportive, is the bedsitter or single flatlet within a building containing similar units for other vulnerable clients, together with a communal room. The added bonus of a motherly figure for a few hours a day to keep an eye on things and to perhaps cook an evening meal is a rare but invaluable provision. Such units and group homes may be run by local authorities, health authorities or by the voluntary sector.

These, then, are the main types of sheltered housing provision that may be available to schizophrenia sufferers in the community. Unfortunately, such provision is but a drop in the ocean and many find themselves living in isolated bedsitters in awesome high-rise flats or in other low-privileged council housing, in dingy unregistered lodgings or in 'bed and breakfast' accommodation.

Sick individuals remain the responsibility of the State, but the taxpayer now meets the cost of providing a profitable business for landladies and property owners instead of the cost of professional care and hospital beds!

DAY CARE

There is nothing approaching an even distribution of such resources throughout the country, but let's take a look at the different types that may be available.

Day Hospitals

These can provide an alternative to in-patient admission. This can be particularly attractive in the case, for example, of a first and possible only breakdown of a young person whose family can continue to provide support at home. In practice, however, there seems to be a tendency to focus more on a new 'worried well' client population, and this may well be the reason why these resources have not become the cornerstone of community care that they were expected to be.

Day Centres

These centres have traditionally been local authority resources providing regular shelter and routine occupation for the chronically mentally ill. Many are widening their brief now to embrace all sorts of stimulating activities and also sessional attendance. As a rule, there is no medical input but nevertheless some of the staff are usually trained and qualified in skills relevant to working with the mentally ill.

Drop-in Centres

These centres tend to be provided by local MIND or NSF groups, sometimes with financial back-up from the local social services department or health authority. The emphasis is on informality; no official referrals are required and anyone with a psychiatric history can wander in and use the facilities. Usually, these include cheap refreshments, somewhere to sit and chat, table games and a darts-board, and suchlike. This type of resource can be very attractive to the type of sufferer who finds those provided by professional agencies too structured and formal.

Evening Clubs

These can be initiated by local voluntary organisations or by several local professionals, or by a combination of both, and successful ones can eventually be run by the members themselves with ongoing back-up support.

Industrial Training Units and Sheltered Workshops

Both these resources provide working conditions similar to those found in factories and other unskilled manual occupational settings. One major difference is that a 'sheltered' situation is provided, where allowance is made for the worker's handicap which may make regular attendance a struggle or maintained concentration difficult. The other major difference is that normal wages will not be paid; the worker will usually be receiving state welfare benefits and will be entitled to nominal bonus payments only. Despite this very real drawback, there is no doubt that such an environment is beneficial to some sufferers in that it provides a structured routine and engenders the feelings of self-respect obtained from 'having a job'. These resources have often been a part of the large old hospitals and unfortunately some are disappearing with them. Of those coming out into the community, some are obliged to become profit-orientated in a way that tends to preclude just the type of schizophrenia sufferer who has benefited from them in the past.

THE ROLE OF DAY-CARE RESOURCES

Where sufferers persevere with attendance at a day-care resource, then they gain the overwhelming advantage of having someone to turn to in times of stress. Voluntary or professional workers are at hand to give advice and day-to-day support. However, what has been described as the 'profound undermining of will-power of the disease'[11] often results in sufferers gradually giving up the effort needed to maintain regular attendance. Because of the scarcity of ready resources, it is equally common for the agencies concerned to let this happen. Thus, there is a twofold problem in supporting the chronically ill schizophrenic patient within the community. Very often there is no appropriate resource available, but even where there is it may equally well be the case that the sufferer lacks the 'get up and go' to persevere with its use. This sort of lack of staying power and motivation is at the very core of the disabling nature of schizophrenia. The worrying thing about even the best-planned resources in the community is that it is assumed that the consumer is well enough to take advantage of them. This is often *not* the case in schizophrenia.

STATE BENEFITS

An example of this sort of problem can be demonstrated in the need to master and understand the complexities of what remains of our welfare state. As we all know, this was intended to provide a system that acted as a 'safety net' for the under-privileged; to many of those concerned, the whole scheme in fact resembles a particularly tricky obstacle race in which you may forfeit your next 'giro' if you stumble! The state benefits system relies on the claimant initiating the procedure, and mentally ill patients often fail at the first hurdle. They do not realise the necessity to supply the Department of Social Security (DSS) with medical certificates *from the start of their illness*. This problem is further aggravated in schizophrenia because sufferers may not be recognised as being sick until months, or even years, after the illness is profoundly affecting their daily functioning and the holding down of employment. Let's take a look at the benefits system as it affects someone with this illness:

Statutory Sick Pay

Since 1986, employers have been responsible for paying this for the first twenty-eight weeks of sick leave. The patient will then automatically qualify for Invalidity Benefit. If the sufferer is unemployed at the time of becoming unwell, or becomes unemployed during the first twenty-eight weeks of sickness, then it is important to obtain medical certificates for the duration of this period and to forward them immediately to the DSS. This will ensure, provided the individual has enough 'paid-up' stamps for the relevant twelve-month working period, that Sickness Benefit will be payable and will, again, lead to qualification for Invalidity Benefit.

Invalidity Benefit

The importance of this benefit is that it is not a *means-tested* one and is therefore unaffected by any change in the financial circumstances of the claimant. It has the added advantage that so long as medical certificates are provided (and this requirement can be covered by an 'indefinite period' certificate where justified) and the claimant's 'sick' status is undisputed by the DSS, then payments are regular and reliable. Finally, the sufferer is entitled to take advantage of the 'therapeutic earnings' rule if claiming this benefit. He or she may earn up to a limit, around half of the full benefit, in part-time work, without penalty. Such work will qualify if the patient's doctor states that it will be therapeutic for him or her and if it meets certain criteria set by the DSS (this must be established before work is started). This can be useful for those schizophrenia sufferers who tend to fluctuate in their ability to work, and who greatly benefit from working during periods of better health.

It is not uncommon to meet sufferers, whose chronic disability is beyond question, but who have lost the right to full Invalidity Benefit because they had run out of the 'paid-up' stamps requirement owing to undue delay in providing medical certificates. Similarly, there are many young sufferers whose illness has prevented them being employed long enough to qualify in this way for Invalidity Benefit. What alternatives are available?

Severe Disablement Allowance (SDA)

It is necessary in most cases to prove an 80 per cent disability before this is payable. There is a detailed structure for measuring physical disability, but none at the time of writing for mental illness. There can be no doubt that some schizophrenia sufferers are 100 per cent disabled when it comes to measuring their ability to work and there should be no difficulty in establishing this. However, it is far less simple with the majority of chronic sufferers, who may indeed be able to work intermittently.

This benefit is subject to the Therapeutic Earnings Rule in the same way as Invalidity Benefit and is payable to anyone who has been incapable of work for 196 days, who either meets the 80 per cent disability requirement, or *is between 16 and 20 years of age*. It is also payable to older individuals who can prove they have been too ill to work since before their twentieth birthday or who receive Mobility or Attendance Allowance.

Attendance Allowance

This is a benefit that some DSS departments find is not claimed so often as might be expected. It is payable to the patient, not to the carer. Some sufferers have successfully claimed this, and qualification depends on satisfying the requirement that 'you must be so severely disabled that for six months you have needed continual supervision throughout the day/night in order to avoid substantial danger to yourself or others'.[12] To put this another way, if someone needs to be around to safeguard the sufferer's interests day or night, or both, then you should be carefully considering this worthwhile benefit. It is two-tiered and may be claimed for daytime hours only or for twenty-four hour cover. There is no reason why relatives should not make the application on behalf of a sufferer if he or she is not well enough to cope with this. On the other hand, any sufferer who really is in need of help and supervision, but *who lives alone, without such help* should note that this is in itself no obstacle to obtaining the allowance; quite the contrary! It is the *need* for supervision that is the vital factor here and the benefit can be claimed in order to pay for appropriate help.

Application is made via leaflet NI 205. In due course, a doctor appointed by the DSS will visit the sufferer at home to assess his or her disability. It may be helpful to enlist the written support of a social worker, CPN, or day-centre staff, to clarify the sort of problems the individual sufferer is encountering as the visiting doctor will not know the claimant and is unlikely to be a specialist in this type of illness. If the application is unsuccessful, it may be useful to learn that around half such claims are eventually awarded on appeal so it may be well worth going ahead with this, with the help, perhaps, of the local Citizens Advice Bureau or the Advisory Officers at the National Schizophrenia Fellowship.

Invalid Care Allowance

This is payable to certain carers of working age with a limited income, who spend at least 35 hours a week looking after an individual who receives Attendance Allowance. Again, this is another benefit which may be worth looking into and it is applied for via leaflet NI 212.

Income Support

This has replaced supplementary benefit and is, therefore, *means tested.* It will not be payable if the claimant has a certain amount of savings and at the time of writing it will be only payable in full if these do not exceed £3,000 and there is no other source of income. Given these conditions, then claimants can go on to earn an extra £5 per week only. This benefit is often the only income available to those sufferers who do not qualify for other benefits, but it can also be a means of topping up an inadequate income from other sources; this could apply to individuals receiving SDA who meet the savings limit requirement for Income Support.

Sufferers claiming Income Support who are unable to work because of their condition should regularly submit medical certificates to the DSS; after six months they will be entitled to a disability premium which at the time of writing will boost their benefit by nearly half as much again and allow an earnings disregard of £15 per week. Again, sufferers gain by obtaining medical certificates and establishing a rightful 'sick status' for the purposes of the benefits scheme.

Importantly, Income Support brings with it a package of other benefits such as help with NHS prescriptions, dental treatment, glasses and fares for hospital treatment and the right to apply for help under the Social Fund.

Social Fund

The old Single Payments which could be claimed for recurring expenses caused by inevitable depreciation of essential items and for emergencies have now been discontinued and replaced by the following two measures:

Community Care Grants

These are intended for helping disabled people to lead independent lives in the community and may therefore be awarded to schizophrenia sufferers leaving hospital, or a similar institution, to help them settle down in the community.

Budgeting Loans

Interest-free loans may be available to cover certain items of furniture and domestic expenses. These loans are only made if the DSS feels the claimant can afford to repay them by deduction from ongoing benefits. They are only worth considering if there is really no way of managing without borrowing money. If this is the case, then one of these interest-free loans is much preferable to borrowing from other more costly sources and certainly better than getting involved with loan sharks!

Housing Benefit

Individuals who receive Income Support qualify for the maximum amount of housing benefit from the local authority. At the present time, this amounts to 100 per cent of the rent and 80 per cent of the Community Charge. Depending on the amount of income derived from various sources, sufferers in similar circumstances but on other benefits will also obtain help with these expenses.

Community Charge (or Poll Tax)

At the time of writing, there are absurd anomalies for the mentally ill in this new system. Most are expected to pay 20 per cent of the local charge but some can claim complete exemption. Such exemption depends on the chronically ill sufferer being in receipt of Invalidity Benefit, Severe Disablement Allowance or Attendance Allowance, and his or her doctor agreeing to confirm in writing that 'the applicant's social functioning and intelligence are severely impaired because of mental illness and that the impairment appears to be permanent'.[13]

Some chronically ill sufferers are refusing to be 'stigmatised' in this way and others are finding their entitlement to exemption depends on the whims of doctors. For example, one NSF member has two sons who are sufferers; the less disabled of the two has been granted exemption, but not his brother. Other members are reporting that in some parts of the country sufferers are being charged *twice*; for living in the family home much of the time (a common occurrence), whilst still maintaining a flat, or whatever.

Meanwhile, while the majority of sufferers in the community seem likely to continue paying 20 per cent of the charge, all those individuals being looked after in residential institutions are to be exempted, so any relatives saving the taxpayer a great deal of money by caring for a sufferer may well feel that they are once again being penalised rather than supported for providing care in the community!

HOW THE BENEFITS SYSTEM WORKS IN PRACTICE

Hopefully, the above discussion provides a guide to what may be available for sufferers. What it may not do is to give any real indication of the frustration and confusion engendered in healthy individuals when they come into contact with the benefits system, let alone its effect on people who are not so fortunate. Whereas many officers in DSS departments are sympathetic in principle to the needs of claimants with severe handicaps, they are often unaware of this particular diagnosis and even less aware of its implications. When all is said and done, it is not uncommon for sufferers themselves to be left in ignorance of their diagnosis and their medical certificates may well state they have 'nervous debility' or something similar. To DSS staff (possibly the most harrassed set of workers in the public sector), who have no training in such matters, schizophrenia sufferers may appear well and able. They cannot be expected to appreciate that it is asking the impossible to expect some of these claimants to sit and wait in a restricted space for twenty minutes, let alone the whole morning or afternoon that a visit to their offices so often involves!

Probably the worst problems occur each and every time claimants change their 'status', by being discharged from hospital, for example, or by completing a training course or giving up work. One father explained:

Specific points in regulations are comparatively easy to discuss. More difficult to get across to someone who has not experienced it is the cumulative effect of trying to sort out the administrative tangles inevitably recurring month after month and year after year, explaining the position (as far as one knows it) to . . . ever-changing officials.[14]

It is not at all unusual for claimants to have to wait for a period of around three weeks for payments of any kind at such times. Inevitably, relatives and friends end up providing the finances to which the individual should be entitled during these periods. What is the sufferer without such support meant to do? Is it any wonder so many slip through the net?

CONCLUSION

Clearly, there are a few excellent resources available, but their availability is patchy to say the least. At best, and when sufferers have the sort of support needed to encourage them to take advantage of such resources, a reasonable quality of life may be attained even by those quite chronically ill. More often, there continues to be little appreciation of the real problems and needs of many sufferers. Where this is the case, then community care is indeed 'family care' and little else.

The next chapter will go on to explore the veritable jungle of the legal system as it applies to mental illness, and to schizophrenia in particular.

6 The Working of the Law

One of the tragedies of this illness is that a small percentage of sufferers inevitably need to be formally admitted to hospital on occasion. Sadly, it is usually those who love them most who have to instigate this trauma. The National Schizophrenia Fellowship comment: 'Great distress is caused for families when sufferers refuse to acknowledge that they are ill, refuse treatment or cannot be persuaded that their delusions *are* delusions.'[1] These families live in dread of the next time they will once again be seen by the sufferer as betraying his or her best interests. It would be very beneficial to everyone concerned if all the professionals involved in obtaining such an admission to hospital were conversant with the loss of insight and contact with reality imposed by the illness. Sadly, this is by no means always the case. On the other hand, although families are horribly aware of such matters, *they* are rarely conversant with the major points of law appertaining to compulsory admission. I hope the information contained in this chapter will help to remedy this situation.

The Mental Health Act 1959 embodied all the optimism of that time, when it was hoped that the advent of neuroleptic drug treatment and the new 'open door' policy would eliminate once and for all the need for the long-term containment of the mentally ill. This has not proved to be the case, although there are now many chronically ill patients able to survive in the community, so long as we continue to have a 'revolving door' policy which caters for their intermittent relapses. In fact, one very positive aspect of the 1959 legislation turned out to be the introduction of the concept of voluntary admission to mental hospitals; by the mid 1970s, nearly 90 per cent of all admissions were on this basis.

By this time, the civil liberties lobby was becoming perturbed about the implication of enforced admission to hospital for the minority of patients so affected. Larry Gostin and other MIND (National Association for Mental Health) workers were the main advocates for the new legislation, which puts much more emphasis on legal rights and less on the need for hospitalised treatment.

The Mental Health Act 1983 is very similar to the 1959 Act, except that the spirit of the law now leans towards the prevention of hospital admission rather than the enablement of hospital admission. This, interestingly, fits in with the overall policy to close down the mental hospitals. There is now a real danger that the decreasing numbers of hospital beds, combined with the aims of this legislation, may bring about a situation where all the rights of the schizophrenic patient are protected except for the right to hospitalisation and treatment. It is a fact of life that none of us is willing to accept medication if we do not believe we are ill; in the two most severe forms of psychosis – the manic stage of manic depressive illness and the acute stage of schizophrenia – the patient has lost touch with reality and is unaware of his or her illness. Surely society has a duty to protect such individuals from these devastating illnesses at such times, and to concentrate on affording them as high a quality of life at other times as is possible? The concept of 'liberty' becomes irrelevant in the former situation and possibly quite inadequate in the latter. Meanwhile, it is already becoming difficult on occasions to obtain voluntary admission to hospital.

THE MENTAL HEALTH ACT 1983

There are five sections under Part II of this legislation which may be of particular interest to schizophrenia sufferers and their families. These are Sections 2, 3, 4, 135 and 136. Each of these may be used to effect the compulsory admission to hospital of a mentally ill patient.

Section 2
The grounds for application are:

> The patient is suffering from mental disorder of a nature or degree which warrants the detention of the patient in a hospital for assessment, or for assessment followed by medical treatment, for at least a limited period and he ought to be so detained in the interests of his own health or safety or with a view to the protection of other persons.[2]

Clearly, then, this section concerns admission to hospital for the purpose of assessment, or for assessment followed by medical treatment as necessary. It lasts for a period of up to twenty-eight days. Application can be made by an approved social worker (ASW) or by the nearest relative (for a definition of this term, see page 70), with the recommendation of two medical practitioners.

The applicant must have seen the patient within a period of fourteen days before the application is made. If the applicant is an ASW, then that officer has a duty to interview the patient personally and a duty to take such steps as are practicable to inform the nearest relative that the application is being made.

The main problem presented by Section 2, insofar as relatives of a schizophrenic patient are concerned, is that the patient is told at the time of admission of his or her right to appeal against this compulsory detention by applying to a Mental Health Review Tribunal within a period of fourteen days following admission. This provision, introduced in the 1983 legislation, has little merit in the eyes of those who manage to obtain help for a sick relative who is temporarily out of touch with reality, only to have him or her presented with such information and the accompanying paperwork on entering the hospital! However, in practice, such procedure is not likely to interfere with the administering of necessary treatment in the first instance. It can, nevertheless, cause further trauma for both patient and family as such tribunals are based on a legal model, not a medical model, and there have already been cases of relatives' comments, supposedly made in confidence to a social worker or a doctor, being revealed to the patient. This can cause irreparable damage to relationships.

NB Tribunals are now common and lawyers, as much as doctors, are determining a patient's needs for treatment. In this context, it is a sad fact that relatives need to beware of expressing any sentiments that they do not want mentioned to the patient.

Relatives must also bear in mind that it is quite possible for a patient to be discharged after a tribunal although they and the doctors know he or she is not yet ready for this and not in touch with reality all the time. This is called protecting the patient's rights! Where there is still a family for the patient to return to, then premature discharge will not help his or her recovery. Where there is no family, then premature discharge can be disastrous.

Section 3
The grounds for application are:

> The patient is suffering from mental illness . . . and his mental disorder is of a nature or degree which makes it appropriate for him to receive medical treatment in a hospital and it is necessary for the health or safety of the patient or for the protection of other persons that he should receive such treatment and it cannot be provided unless he is detained under this section.[3]

Clearly, then, this section concerns admission for the purpose of treatment; it lasts for a period of up to six months. Application can be made by an ASW or the patient's nearest relative; either must have seen the patient within a period of fourteen days of the application being made, and the application must have the recommendation of two medical practitioners. An ASW cannot make application under this section if the nearest relative is opposed to this.

Some social services departments are very loath to use Section 3 at the present time, preferring to take the least restrictive action possible and seeing the clause 'and it cannot be provided unless he is detained under this section' as justification for this. However, the law seems to be quite clear in that Section 2 (discussed above) is intended primarily for assessment, with treatment to follow as appropriate, and this can scarcely apply when the patient's condition is well known to the hospital doctors. Where this is the case, then the 'treatment' section should be the one of choice. This allows more time for such treatment and need be no more restrictive than is absolutely necessary as the patient can be discharged before the six-month period is ended. Again, the use of Section 3 in its proper context can be more beneficial to the patient and the family by avoiding premature discharge, and it also allows time for the professionals concerned to make proper provision for the patient's after-care.

NB The use of Section 3 implies a duty by the local health authority or the local authority social services department to provide after-care for the patient after discharge from hospital, and discharge or completion of the section.

Section 4

This section is for the purpose of assessment in emergency; it lasts for seventy-two hours only. Application may be made by an ASW or the patient's nearest relative, with the recommendation of just one medical practitioner; wherever possible this should be a doctor who knows the patient well. The applicant must have seen the patient within a period of twenty-four hours of the application being made.

Section 29 of the 1959 Mental Health Act, now Section 4 in the new legislation, was much abused and used far more than was warranted. It was seen as the easiest way to arrange a formal admission, with only one doctor being required, and the responsibility then left to the hospital medical team to extend the section once the patient was safely in hospital. The new legislation, quite rightly, discourages this practice; Section 4 should *not* be used unless the urgency is such that it is impracticable to wait for the opinion of another medical practitioner. Formal admission is rarely accomplished without trauma for all concerned and it is not justifiable unless there is obvious need for assessment and/or treatment; this being the case, then those responsible for making the application should carry out the work properly.

NB If there is no dire urgency, then the applicant should insist on a second medical practitioner being sent for. Whether or not the nearest relative is the applicant, it is almost certainly in the patient's and the family's interests that good practice is insisted upon at this point.

Section 135
An ASW may give information on oath before a Justice of the Peace if there is reasonable cause to suspect that a person believed to be suffering from mental disorder has been ill-treated or neglected or not kept under proper control or is unable to care for him- or herself and is living alone. A warrant can be granted and a police constable can then enter the premises, accompanied by a doctor and an ASW.

Section 136
The police may use this section if they find an individual in a 'public place' who seems to be suffering from mental disorder and is in immediate need of care or control. They may take the patient to a 'place of safety' (usually a hospital, a local authority home or a police station). The purpose of this is to enable an assessment to be made by a doctor and ASW, and the detention may not exceed seventy-two hours.

GUARDIANSHIP ORDER

This is another option available to social services departments and nearest relatives, where perhaps some sort of restraint is necessary to protect a patient's interests.

A patient of sixteen years or over can be received into guardianship; the maximum duration is six months, but this can then be renewed for a further six months, and then for one year at a time. The nearest relative can apply, as can an ASW (but only with the agreement of the nearest relative). The recommendations of two medical practitioners are required.

The effect of a Guardianship Order is that the guardian has the power to require the patient to live in a specified place and to attend specified places for the purposes of medical treatment, occupation, education or training. He or she can also require access to the patient to be given to any doctor, ASW or other specified person.

NB This is a little-used option at the present time, but it might well prove to be an acceptable alternative to hospitalisation in some cases of schizophrenia.

NEAREST RELATIVES

It will be evident from the above notes that the nearest relative may hold a key role in the formal admission of a patient under the Mental Health Act. There are clear guidelines on determining the nearest relative. The following list gives the order of priority:

husband or wife	grandparent
son or daughter	grandchild
father or mother	uncle or aunt
brother or sister	nephew or niece

The Act states that:

> . . . in deducing relationships for the purposes of this section, any relationship of the half-blood shall be treated as a relationship of the whole blood, and an illegitimate person shall be treated as the legitimate child of his mother.[4]

Where two relatives have equal priority, then the elder of the two, **regardless of sex**, will be the choice, and half-blood relationships will take second place. Where the patient normally resides with a relative, then that relative will be the 'nearest relative'; if the patient normally resides with more than one relative, then the list above will indicate which of those is the 'nearest relative'. However, if the patient has lived with a *non*-relative as husband or wife for **at least six months** prior to admission to hospital, then that person is considered to be the nearest relative. If the patient has lived with a non-relative, but not as husband or wife, for **five years**, then the person is considered to be a **relative**, but not necessarily the 'nearest relative'.

An application can be made by any relative, or by any person living with the patient prior to admission, or by an ASW, to the county court for a displacement order to be made. The court can then appoint the applicant or other suitable person to act as the 'nearest relative' if it can be proved that the nearest relative is incompetent, or acts unreasonably without due regard to the interests of the patient or others.

Nearest relatives have several powers under Part II of the Act, apart from the right to make application for hospital admission. Under Section

13(4), they can require an ASW to consider making application for hospital admission:

> It shall be the duty of a local social services authority if so required by the nearest relative of a patient residing in their area, to direct an approved social worker as soon as practicable to take the patient's case into consideration . . . with a view to making an application for his admission to hospital; and if in any such case that approved social worker decides not to make an application he shall inform the nearest relative of his reasons in writing.[5]

Nearest relatives can also make an order for discharge in respect of a patient admitted for assessment or treatment or where the patient is the subject of guardianship. Although other relatives concerned with the patient do not share these powers, their expressed views have to be taken into account before an ASW makes application for admission of the patient.

Although the National Schizophrenia Fellowship quite justifiably fought for the right of the nearest relative to continue to have the power to make application for admission, it is the writer's experience that many relatives 'fight shy' of the responsibility of making this move. This is understandable as the family naturally wants to maintain as good a relationship as possible with the patient and they do not want to feel that they have 'put him (or her) away'. However, there is a tendency for blame to then be attached to an ASW for also declining to make an application. Perhaps it would be helpful at this stage to quote Larry Gostin's interpretation of the ASW's role in this connection: 'the principle of avoiding admission to hospital wherever possible, and of returning hospitalised patients to the community, should become the focus of the social worker's role under the 1983 Act.'[6] He also mentions consideration of alternative measures such as investigation of 'the least restrictive treatment and care settings, crisis intervention and management, as well as support for the patient and his family'.[7]

Clearly, the ASW may well believe that it is his or her duty to avoid an admission to hospital wherever possible, and this viewpoint is, regrettably, defensible in the present climate but *only* if alternative measures are taken which include satisfying the immediate need for treatment and support for the patient and the family. Thus, the family may, and should, demand such services but they cannot demand that the ASW makes application for admission to hospital. For this reason, the family may have to decide between accepting any alternative measures offered or making an application independently of the ASW, and with the support of medical practitioners. In this case, the ASW will provide the necessary documents for completion and will explain the appropriate procedure.

However, it may be that the ASW is not fully conversant with the course of this particular illness, albeit the one most catered for under the legislation. For this reason, it may be useful for the nearest relative to point out that the grounds for admission under Sections 2 and 3 include the words 'health or safety'. It would be a foolish person who was prepared to predict the acts and behaviour of an individual suffering a schizophrenic breakdown or relapse, so no one can guarantee his or her safety. Insofar as 'health' is concerned, there is a discussion in Chapter 1 and another in Chapter 4 on the dangers of allowing a schizophrenic illness to proceed untreated.

Occasionally, it may prove impossible to obtain the services of an ASW promptly, for example at night-time (if the social services department do not provide a telephone number for emergency calls, try telephoning the police or local hospital for ways of reaching the duty social worker), and it may be best under these circumstances to call the police if there is any violence, or threat of violence. Families afflicted with the illness are often loud in their praise of the way the police handle such emergencies.

CRIMINAL PROCEEDINGS

There has been no attempt in this discussion to explore in detail the criminal law as it relates to the mentally ill. Suffice it to say that ample provisions have been made in the *legislation* for the treatment of mentally ill offenders rather than simply containing them in prison. In *practice*, however, there are not enough hospital beds to meet the demand. Cutbacks in spending have led to hospitals dispensing with plans for local secure units which could cater for such offenders and the expected growth of such services has been painfully slow.

Courts do not always, by any means, use their powers to seek hospitalisation or similar treatment for offenders. Where they do, it is often dependent upon doctors accepting these patients; this in turn is dependent upon the doctors having the necessary facilities, and in many cases these are not available. It is not surprising that mentally ill offenders often go to prison; it is, however, very disturbing and an indictment on our 'civilised' society. Where patients are directed to special hospitals, such as Broadmoor, this can be extremely hard on both patient and family. Relatives often live hundreds of miles away and this causes additional suffering.

It may be worth underlining the fact, at this stage, that many families suffer nightmarish fears that their schizophrenic relative may commit an offence during an untreated relapse. This is a valid fear and one that can motivate a determination in the family to obtain hospitalisation for the patient when an 'outsider' may misunderstand such fears and think that no such seemingly drastic action is justified.

THE MENTAL HEALTH ACT COMMISSION

This is made up of members of the various health care professions, the legal professions and lay-people, all contributing in a part-time capacity. The Commission is intended to be a 'watch-dog' and it will arrange to visit local and special hospitals, to interview detained patients and to investigate any complaints by them. It also investigates any complaints about the exercising of powers and duties under the Mental Health Act 1983. Another of its responsibilities is concerned with monitoring the effectiveness of the new Code of Practice laid before Parliament at the end of 1989.

THE CODE OF PRACTICE

This long-awaited document has on the whole been well-received by the various bodies concerned with the mentally ill. Two previous attempts failed this test and had to be abandoned. One immediate concern of the National Schizophrenia Fellowship has been taken aboard by the Department of Health and is being rectified. This was that the new code did not make it clear that if an ASW declines to make an application for compulsory admission, or if there is not one available to do so, then the nearest relative should be advised of his or her right to make the application (with the appropriate medical recommendations) and receive guidance on how to proceed with this.

The fellowship's concern over two other issues has been submitted to the department for further consideration. The first is the code's seeming emphasis on protecting patients' freedom within the hospital setting, rather than any clear and practical directions on curtailing that freedom. This comes at a time when the NSF increasingly receives reports of very sick, sectioned patients walking out of hospital with dire results for their own or others' safety. The code suggests that patients should not be deprived of their daytime clothing – though this is an accepted and recognised signal to others and to themselves that they are not yet well enough to wander outside (and one that many recovered sufferers acknowledge with gratitude) – and recommends a cumbersome and complicated procedure to be undertaken by any nurse who undertakes to lock the ward doors. These sort of directions make it easier for hard-pressed nurses to let patients at risk wander off rather than restrict their freedom.

The second concern is the failure of the code to address itself to the problems caused by the widespread mistaken belief amongst professionals working with the legislation that individuals have to be a danger to themselves or others before they can be compulsorily admitted to hospital. It is a common occurrence to hear the comment, 'he is very ill, but unfortunately he is not sectionable yet'. In fact, the legislation does allow, of course, for admission on health grounds alone. This is very important in schizophrenia, when some patients can remain distressingly sick and unable to function normally without deteriorating to the point of apparent danger to themselves or others. Others can become irreversibly damaged by continuing unrelieved psychotic symptoms.

I believe that this Code has a great deal to offer in the way of detailed advice and guidance for good professional practice, and will do much to alleviate unnecessary suffering if important factors such as these can be accommodated. If this does not happen, then I suspect that the provision of a lengthy and comprehensive Code of Practice will have little impact on the worst abuses and tragedies that occur with this illness.

COMMUNITY TREATMENT ORDERS

Under the Mental Health Act of 1959 it was possible to discharge patients on a six-month section back into the community and to renew the section as necessary. In this way, a small but important group of schizophrenia sufferers could be maintained in the community. There is no such provision under the current legislation. The sufferers most affected are the ones who respond quite dramatically to the neuroleptic drugs but who never seem to gain insight into this. They tend to discontinue the medication as soon as they are discharged from hospital, and start to deteriorate at that point or shortly afterwards. This vicious circle is a painful one for the sufferers who are aware of their real potential to achieve but nevertheless experience one failure after another because they cannot function properly. It is similarly painful for those who love them and for other members of the community who become involved in the individual's downward spiral of torment and despair. Eventually, this leads to the trauma of a compulsory admission to hospital and the cycle starts again.

For the past few years a debate has ranged on this subject between all the different factions that make up the mental health lobby. Proposals for some sort of Community Treatment Order have been rejected by many as a violation of civil liberties, and by others as impractical. The fact that the renewing of six-month sections in the community worked very well in the past is ignored. Suggestions that Guardianship Orders could be used to persuade these individuals to comply with their drug regimes are criticised on the grounds that they 'have no teeth', which is certainly true in their present form. Meanwhile, the avoidable wastage of lives and the resultant misery continues unabated.

So, as we come to the end of Part I, we have covered many of the basic facts about a schizophrenic illness. The rest of the book attempts to answer the question: 'What can we do about it?'

PART II
Especially for families

7 Diagnosis and Professional Care

Everyday life in your household is turning into a nightmare; a relative is becoming unrecognisable, probably hostile and withdrawn. If there has been a dramatic change of personality, however insidious its development, with no recognisable illness or significant change of environment, then schizophrenia may well be the cause. If so, an early diagnosis is highly desirable; you do not want to wait for a complete breakdown of personality, with all the risk, trauma and stigma involved. Breakdown can lead to a situation in which the patient can become so confused and terrified that he or she is really at risk. It also brings with it the danger of irreversible damage.[1,2]

OBTAINING HELP

So, something has to be done! This decided, you may now find yourself in a 'mad hatter's tea party' situation where the patient's denial of any illness is matched by the medical profession's reluctance to diagnose one. This attitude has contributed to, and is reinforced by, the secrecy and stigma attached to schizophrenia. Despite the fact that one in a hundred people contract this illness, doctors are resistant when relatives describe classic symptoms in their loved ones. You need to be aware of this and also of the possibility that your initial approach for help may be interpreted as the needless anxiety of a neurotic parent, the lack of understanding of parents about the problems of adolescence (however healthy the rest of your grown-up offspring!), the gripings of a frustrated and neglected wife or the rantings of an over-demanding husband. Maybe for the first time in your life, your intentions will become suspect.

Meanwhile, be prepared! Perhaps due to an excess of adrenalin in the face of danger, combined with the innate instinct of humans for survival, the patient will suddenly demonstrate normality and good health in front of the doctor, becoming affable, reasonable and, more importantly, plausible. On the other hand, you will be shattered by this turn of events and, after weeks or months of increasing anxiety, it may be you who is seen as the more likely patient. Make no mistake about it, healthy people behave quite abnormally in crisis situations; this is one of the factors that led mistakenly to the acceptance of dangerous theories in the 1960s that the sick family scapegoats one of its members, presenting this individual as the patient. It is not really surprising, therefore, that families' first attempts to obtain help often fail. Tragically, treatment is then delayed for weeks, months or, in some cases years.

Forewarned, then, is forearmed and it would be a good idea to write to your GP before seeking an appointment, detailing the problems you are experiencing with your relative and carefully describing the changes in his or her personality and behaviour over the past weeks, months or years. Keep a copy of this letter for future reference.

If you find that your GP will not take your plight seriously, or if the patient is referred to a psychiatrist who diagnoses 'a mild adolescent disturbance' or whatever (as so often happens), what can you do next? If your efforts have resulted in no improvement in the patient's condition, then it may well be a good idea to approach one of the self-help organisations such as the National Schizophrenia Fellowship or the Schizophrenia Association of Great Britain (see list of useful addresses at the end of the book), and describe to them what is happening to you. They should be able to advise you and perhaps put you in touch with other families with a sufferer. Discussing your own experiences and hearing about theirs should clarify the situation for you and enable you to return to your doctor with more confidence, requesting a first (or second) referral for psychiatric assessment. Be firm about this; you have nothing to lose and your family's future is at stake . . .

There is one further obstacle that you may meet. You could be unlucky and find yourself dealing with a psychiatrist who refuses to discuss a patient over eighteen years of age with relatives, unless the patient is present. It takes little imagination to envisage the bizarre quality of an interview between doctor, patient and relatives with the patient behaving inexplicably normally and the family trying to convey its desperate concern without further angering or seeming disloyal to their relative.

The grounds for such professional practice are based on the principle that an adult is responsible for his or her own actions and well-being and is entitled to protection from the violation of these rights by relatives and others. Such worthy ideas are patently nonsense in the face of an illness which, by definition, divorces the patient from reality and often causes its victims to be paranoid about loved ones. Fortunately, the practice does not seem to be as common these days as it used to be, but if you do come across it, you may wish to seek a second opinion before the patient becomes attached to this doctor. The latter is unlikely to see the need for including you, the family, in future treatment plans and will not have the benefit of learning about the family's needs or any problems you may experience in trying to support the patient in the community. Under these circumstances, neither the patient's nor the family's best interests can be served.

Alternatively, you might like to discuss with such a psychiatrist an extract from a recent report of the Interdisciplinary Working Party convened by the Royal College of Psychiatrists and contained in Appendix II.

A DIAGNOSIS

Let's now assume that your perseverance has been rewarded and a psychiatric referral has resulted in a straightforward diagnosis, with the overwhelming advantages this brings. Now you have an explanation for the nightmare you have all been experiencing; you have access to the organisations that exist just to help sufferers and their families, and to all the up-to-date literature on schizophrenia. Above all, the sufferer has access to treatment with the neuroleptic drugs that have changed the face of this illness for so many of its victims.

NEUROLEPTIC DRUG TREATMENT

In Chapter 4 we discussed the fact that many patients respond very quickly indeed to these drugs. You may find that your relative obtains some relief from his or her torturous thoughts almost immediately, due in part to the sedative content of the medication. It will take longer for the psychotic nightmare to begin to fade, but a real improvement can usually be seen within two to three weeks. If there is no real 'let-up' in the patient's distress, then it is usual for the amount of medication to be increased accordingly. It may be that in some cases another neuroleptic drug will be prescribed, as every individual responds differently to the various drugs although they all have similar properties.

The initial monitoring and adjusting of the patient's medication may be the main deciding factor in his or her recovery. Some doctors are very cautious in the amounts they prescribe and some are frankly ambivalent about the drugs in the first place. Clearly, very few people would wish that patients should be needlessly 'drugged-up', but it is a sad irony that some individuals remain tortured and unwell until a change to a doctor who recognises their need for an increased dose or change of neuroleptic medication. Most people appreciate that one ounce of alcohol can affect all of us differently because of each individual's unique chemistry; the same logic is not always applied to the administering of drugs for a schizophrenic illness. I have known patients who would seem to have suffered further and avoidable damage for long periods because of inadequate drug treatment. Fuller Torrey, a leading psychiatrist in the United States, reports that he has seen more cases of under-medication than of over-medication.[3] There can be little remaining doubt that for an acute schizophrenic illness, the prescribing of the right neuroleptic drug in the right amount, earlier rather than later, is the essence of effective treatment. Similarly, the monitoring of the medication and continued prescription of a dose *that enables the sufferer to function properly* is the essence of a good prognosis. It should always be worthwhile to ask for a second opinion from a psychiatrist who sees this type of illness primarily as a chemical imbalance if the sufferer shows no improvement on drug treatment.

Tragically, for a small minority of the sufferers with these positive-type symptoms, neuroleptic drugs are not the answer. Some cannot tolerate them, even with antidote medication for side-effects, and others obtain no real relief. As yet, we have no adequate answer for the torment of these patients. However, other drugs that can help in some cases are those that relieve depression and also Carbamazepine and Lithium, the most popular forms of treatment for the mood changes of a manic depressive illness.

If the patient has responded positively to medication, then count your blessings and make sure the treatment continues in the foreseeable future. Neuroleptic drugs must be taken regularly if they are to provide effective cover and it is essential that an injection or daily dose of tablets should not be overlooked. In the early days of recovery, relapse can be sudden and devastating. At a later stage, attempts to decrease the dose or withdraw the medication should only be undertaken under careful medical supervision. Meanwhile the patient will need monitoring for possible side-effects; these range from blurred vision and skin rashes to the Parkinsonian-type symptoms of trembling, edginess, aching legs, excessive restlessness and, more rarely, a frightening stiffness with lock-jaw and rolling back of the eyes. Antidote medication should only be taken if signs of any of the relevant symptoms appear, but it is usually a good idea to have a prescription available during the first week or so, for use only in emergency, as it is not reasonable to expect patients to comply with taking medication in the future if they have an early unforgettable trauma with dramatic side-effects.

HOSPITALISATION?

Increasingly, it is becoming possible for an acute schizophrenic break-down to be treated outside of hospital. Clearly, it may be an advantage for the patient to stay at home if at all possible, so long as this is not attempted for all the wrong reasons. Sometimes too much emphasis may be put on avoiding the stigma of psychiatric inpatient treatment on the sufferer's record, when in fact this has less significance than the diagnosis itself. Similarly, a family's feelings about their relative going into one of 'those hospitals' or 'those wards' may be paramount, at the expense of appreciating that such places can provide the asylum that the sick person may desperately need at this time. For many, but not for all, the feeling of safety provided by such asylum can result in an immediate, albeit temporary, improvement in their condition. This aptly demonstrates the protective environment that a short stay in hospital can provide at such a time.

For those individuals who do have the option of staying at home, this can be beneficial so long as those caring for them have the tremendous resources needed to cope with the patient's fears and with what may be unremitting torment for days, or for a lot longer. They will need to provide constant company and supervision around the clock for the psychotic sufferer, unless immediate 'day-care' is made available. This, of course, can give the family a break from an exhausting emotional strain and the sufferer a diversion from his or her tortured thoughts.

When sufferers go into hospital for a psychotic breakdown nowadays, the chances are that they will be discharged in a matter of weeks, once the medication can be seen to be working effectively, and often long before recovery is complete. This means that those at home quickly have to become very skilled at providing understanding and support if their relative is to thrive and recover as much quality of life as possible. This important subject is discussed in detail in the next chapter, but meanwhile how can carers best make sure that they have the professional backing they need if they are to succeed in this task?

AFTER-CARE

The first priority is to establish lines of communication with the professional team which has been supervising the patient's health. Your priority must be to establish with the psychiatrist his or her proposed plans for the sufferer's after-care before discharge takes place. This is the time to do this, before you find yourselves out there on your own! If injections have not been prescribed, then it may be that nothing more is contemplated than occasional follow-up sessions at an out-patient's clinic. If this is the case, you would be well advised to ask for a professional, such as a community psychiatric nurse, to monitor your relative's medication and to answer the queries that are bound to crop up in the aftermath of a schizophrenic breakdown. As no-one, *but no-one*, can tell whether or not the sufferer will be at risk of further breakdown, relatives should not be fobbed off with reassurances that this sort of professional backing will not be needed. It is not at all uncommon for patients to receive effective treatment following their diagnosis, demonstrating therefore that they have an excellent potential for a real recovery, only to relapse again in the absence of follow-up supervision. This is clearly not acceptable practice and families must ensure that there is a professional who will respond to a call for help from either the sufferer or the family. This last is the minimum requirement if the patient is to remain stable and make progress. He or she will have setbacks along the way, particularly in the early days, and you will need skilled help at such times, as well as moral support! Do have faith in your own judgment. Recent research by Max Birchwood and his fellow clinical psychologists at Birmingham has confirmed what families have always known: relatives do notice early signs of relapse in the sufferer before others do. It is important that this is recognised, as there is usually only a very brief period during which the sufferer's co-operation can be won and relapse avoided. It is crucial therefore that help should be sought earlier rather than later and that professionals should listen and respond when those closest to the sufferer report these first warning signs.

In the next chapter, we will look at ways in which relatives and friends can help sufferers to recover as much as possible of their old potential.

8 Understanding and Support

Let us assume that your relative has now been diagnosed and is receiving appropriate treatment. The patient is at home, but probably not well enough, for the time being at least, to resume previous responsibilities. Nevertheless, he or she seems a lot better and any bizarre symptoms may well have disappeared. Having said that, it is quite possible that any or all of the following are still in evidence:

- Apathy; no real interest in anything.
- Lethargy; overwhelming tiredness; just sits around all day.
- Difficult, if not impossible, to get up in the morning.
- Apparently content to sleep for hours on end, but quite wakeful by your bedtime.
- Tends to want to play noisy music most of the night.
- Intent on eating enormous quantities of junk food and drinking endless cups of tea or coffee (together with cigarettes, if previously a smoker).
- Regression of table manners. Shovelling of food into mouth, as if half-starved.
- Whilst excessively self-conscious in some ways, seemingly uninterested about others' opinions; neglectful of personal hygiene and appearance; quite resentful if this is mentioned.
- Overt over-dependency upon another, often Mum.
- Can be very demanding and seemingly unaware of others' needs.
- Deterioration around monthly period times for female patients.
- Strange ideas and distorted perceptions still around.
- Paranoid ideas, particularly about you.
- Obsession about wanting to stop taking medication, which is blamed for all remaining symptoms.

Before you are tempted to come to the conclusion that this is 'bloody-minded' behaviour rather than sickness, may I introduce you to my two Golden Rules?

1. Recognise the patient's sickness Give him or her the dignity of a 'sick' role, which recognises impairment beyond the sufferer's control. This does not imply any need to pamper or indulge; it implies respect.

2. Acceptance Accept the patient *where he or she is now*; try to avoid the temptation to contrast previous potential with present potential. Many parents and spouses are faced with the need to adjust their sights when offspring or partner can no longer fulfil former ambitions or career potential. This is probably the saddest and most difficult adjustment families have to make; how much worse this must be for the patient.

Bearing in mind these two Golden Rules, let us now consider what is behind the sort of behaviour listed at the beginning of this chapter. Sometimes it is easier to contend with difficult behaviour if we can find a reason for it. Usually, we tend to judge others' behaviour by our own. This rarely leads to a clearer understanding of our 'fellow man'; it will achieve nothing at all if we apply this measurement to a schizophrenia sufferer. Our own behaviour and our own experiences do not 'fit' unless we suffer the same sort of symptoms ourselves! Let us look at the sort of behaviour mentioned earlier in the light of our understanding, albeit limited, of these symptoms.

Firstly, schizophrenia *breeds* lethargy and apathy. You may have experienced similar feelings following a genuine bout of influenza – feeling exhausted and flat however much rest you've taken. This is very real and it has nothing to do with idleness. Many illnesses cause such symptoms, but with schizophrenia it is too easy to look at an able-bodied young person and assume that laziness is the cause of the inertia. The remedy is ensuring the patient does have adequate rest, but providing enough stimulation during waking hours. You will need to be patient; progress will be slow. The subject of stimulation is discussed in Chapter 9.

Restlessness and inability to concentrate are symptoms of the illness, but it is only fair to comment that these can be aggravated by the neuroleptic drugs. Nevertheless, as good health returns, albeit very gradually, powers of concentration should improve. Meanwhile, it is helpful to provide opportunities for modest attempts at, say, watching a previously enjoyed television comedy series, but do not expect too much at first.

Difficulty in waking up in the morning (whether or not the patient has had much sleep during the night) is a classic symptom of many schizophrenia sufferers. It is my belief that diet can be an influencing factor here – see Chapters 10 and 11. Meanwhile, if you doubt the genuine nature of this difficulty (laziness again?), try dragging the patient out of bed and watch him or her fall into a stupor shortly afterwards, virtually sleeping standing up. You will probably have noticed this syndrome long before diagnosis was obtained; the patient turns night into day. Gradual improvement in health brings about an equally gradual return to normality here, but *do* try dietary treatment, as an inability to get up and function in the morning can be a real handicap in trying to resume a normal routine.

The obsession with junk foods and stimulants is dealt with in detail in Chapters 10 and 11. I believe that any regression of table manners is also influenced for the better by adjustment of diet.

Self-consciousness is an entrenched part of the illness. Patients describe themselves as resembling 'a shining beacon', for example, and feel appropriately conspicuous and remarkable. It is interesting, therefore, that some do not seem to even consider the sort of things about which other people are self-conscious; personal hygiene, care of appearance, etc. This is a source of considerable frustration and discomfort to many families and it may be helpful to provide some sort of explanation for this anomaly. Some patients work very hard at minimising their self-awareness; they hate themselves and studiously avoid looking in mirrors or paying any attention whatsoever to their bodies. Others have delusions about washing and bathing. Where neither of these considerations applies, the overwhelming lethargy experienced by some patients provokes a similar contempt for such trivial matters as washing as that demonstrated by many children. Clearly there is a need for some sort of compromise that is acceptable to all concerned and this tricky subject is discussed under 'give and take' measures later in the chapter.

EMOTIONAL DEPENDENCY

Over-dependency upon another, trusted person, will be something that most families will be well acquainted with by the time of the diagnosis. This will usually, but not always, be focused on the patient's mother, and the patient may well seem to resent other members of the family as intruders on this relationship. This close attachment to the mother contributed to theories in the 1960s and 1970s about unhealthy relationships leading to the illness. This is another 'chicken and egg' situation; many mothers can remember a time when the patient was independent of her in the normal way and related happily to peers. Some of these mothers are rewarded by watching this healthy state of affairs eventually return. Meanwhile, the 'chosen prop' needs to provide patient and understanding support, whilst firmly resisting any attempts to be 'sucked down' into the illness. (I quote a phrase used by several mothers.)

Over-demanding behaviour and a disregard for others' needs are typical traits of people who are not really well; just think of other members of your family confined to bed with some mild ailment! Unfortunately, recovery from schizophrenia is sometimes a long haul and it is not really acceptable for this sort of behaviour to persist indefinitely. This is discussed again later in the chapter.

It is not surprising that an illness that often manifests itself at times of hormonal change tends to worsen during and just before monthly periods. As you may well have noticed prior to diagnosis, schizophrenia often interrupts the menstrual cycle anyway. It is useful to bear in mind the point that the female patient may be less well at these times. It helps her if she is aware of the connection if this is in fact the case.

The persistence of strange ideas and delusions can be a problem for both the patient and the family. This is discussed later in the chapter, as is the question of any remaining paranoid ideas.

Finally, it is common, almost universal, for the patient to initially blame the medication for remaining symptoms. Few people like taking drugs of any kind and, remember, the schizophrenic patient often feels that he or she has no illness. The drugs are no different from others in that they can cause all sorts of side-effects and patients often resent these and other effects which are in fact caused by the illness. It is natural to assume that lethargy is due to medication, for example. It is helpful if you bear this in mind, whilst resisting the temptation to collude with the patient's wish to give up the medication. For further discussions of this point, see Chapters 4 and 7.

So much for the patient's behaviour. What about everyone else? We all have our own needs. Brothers and sisters, for example, are not usually amused by odd behaviour or, in fact, any behaviour that is different from the 'norm' expected by their friends and colleagues. They are likely to be embarrassed on the one hand and resentful on the other, particularly as so much extra attention is bestowed on this member of the household. Sometimes it has already become clear that brothers and sisters feel like this, when a patient has complained bitterly of 'aggro' at home, but I find it helpful to talk with these young people in any event and point out that this is a *family* illness. There is a genetic component, but not one that is straightforward and predictable. They, therefore, are the lucky ones in that they share the same genes as the patient, but have not contracted this awful disease, which causes the behaviour they resent. It has been my experience that brothers and sisters may be very supportive, even protective, if the illness is discussed in this matter-of-fact fashion.

This said, it is clear that a patient may be exhibiting all of the characteristics outlined at the beginning of the chapter, but the rest of the family have to survive. I advise that certain basic house rules should be agreed, from the start, and here are some suggestions:

1. It is not in the interests of the patient to be allowed to stay in bed all day. A reasonable timetable will need to be provided (this is discussed in Chapter 9) and meals will be eaten with the family as a general rule.
2. Continued eating of junk foods and stimulants aggravate the illness and the patient should be encouraged to eat a health-giving diet, following the suggestions contained in Chapters 10 and 11. This may mean that the patient and the rest of the family must be prepared to change their eating habits.
3. If applicable, minimum standards of personal hygiene must be maintained. It is helpful to reach agreement on these from the start and then insist they be met. Beyond this, it is a mistake to put emphasis on this frustrating subject. By all means be firm if necessary, but do not resort to 'nagging'; it doesn't work with children and is frequently interpreted as hostile criticism by schizophrenic patients.
4. Whilst an overwhelming need to lean on one person is clear and accepted, this must not be allowed to become too unhealthy a dependence. If it does, the patient will demand more and more of that individual's attention, to the exclusion of all others. This will *not* help him or her move towards healthy relationships and resumption of a normal way of life.
5. If the patient suffers a lot of frustration and tends to be disruptive, then I believe it is helpful to everyone concerned for boundaries to be set. It is not beneficial for the patient to feel powerful in this direction and it is certainly not conducive to harmony in the home. Rarely, one finds a patient in the community ruling the household by terror (although this is not necessarily acknowledged) and this can only happen if the family encourages it, albeit unwittingly, and if treatment is inadequate. This is not acceptable and help should be sought at the first signs of any such development. (See Chapter 6.)
6. A similar, but more common, problem is the question of collusion over the illness. It should be clarified from the start that any signs of relapse or refusal to take medication will be discussed openly with the professional(s) concerned with the patient. If this attitude is established from the word go, then the family will feel less pressurised by conflicts of loyalty when needing help.
7. Finally, I suspect that the patient might well wish to lay down one or

two rules. No doubt he or she will demand the right to have privacy and 'space' and this is very important indeed. If wakeful at night, the right to stay up during those anti-social hours may also be required; this is reasonable, but should not include the right to play noisy records or to stomp around waking up the rest of the household.

I hope it is clear from the above suggestions that the same guidelines apply here as those followed by good parents of teenage children. A patient recovering from schizophrenia is an adult and deserves to be treated as one, but the illness can cause symptoms which provoke difficult behaviour. 'Give and take' is the name of the game, but clear boundaries will enable the family to be supportive without resorting to constant nagging and destructive criticism. Nevertheless, there will be times when the patient will be frustrated by relatives' lack of understanding and there will be times when the family will be exasperated and angry. This is no different from the normal course of events in any other household, but your family have more excuse for tempers becoming frayed sometimes. Don't let that worry you too much; if the schizophrenia sufferer is aware that he or she has your respect most of the time, the odd eruption will be a timely reminder that you are all human.

MARRIAGE AND SCHIZOPHRENIA

There are added complications when the sufferer is married and, even more so, a parent. We have discussed the provision of understanding and support within a framework of 'give and take', with house rules as and when necessary. This approach is near enough the usual model with a 'child' of the household for it to be acceptable to the young patient. It is clearly less acceptable to husband or wife, father or mother. Nevertheless, the principle remains the same. The patient with more responsibilities is no less handicapped because of this. The important thing is that any 'rules' should be focused on 'the illness', rather than on 'behaviour' as such. For example, your spouse's symptoms may cause a level of frustration which makes it acceptable to you (albeit unwelcome) for him or her to use bad language occasionally. However, you establish that this will not be acceptable in front of the children, or in company, or whatever. In much the same way, it is possible to reach a compromise over the entertaining of friends, for example. You may wish to protect your partner from the trauma of coping with visitors, but have to insist that the unexpected caller is not rebuffed; you make it easier for your spouse and make it clear that you need support in return.

Clearly, it can be very much more demanding to be married to an ill person than to be the parent of one. Most individuals marry for support and companionship and for a mutually rewarding sex life. All of these positive ingredients of marriage come under threat if one partner develops schizophrenia. Many such marriages do survive and some sufferers seem to flourish with the help of a supportive partner. No doubt the spouse in these cases is basically a strong personality who can make boundaries without undermining the sufferer's self-respect. Nevertheless, it is a tough proposition for both, and often a lonely one for the healthy partner. If he or she lacks a kindly shoulder to lean on, I would strongly recommend joining a self-help group such as those run by members of the National Schizophrenia Fellowship. Where there are young children of the marriage, then it is likely that social work support will be available if this is requested. The whole subject of survival of the marriage of a sufferer is worthy of a book of its own and there is not space here to do it justice. Suffice it to say that marriages only survive if the severity of the illness is not too great to allow for some give and take; given this, they are likely to survive only if both partners are determined to salvage the marriage and if the illness allows them to maintain some measure of mutual respect.

REALITY TESTING

I would now like to consider the problems caused by lingering symptoms of the illness which are not always apparent to the onlooker. Dealing with these in a way that enables the patient to live with them is an important part of finding the road to recovery. It is very likely indeed that long after the patient seems to have a firm grasp of reality and appears well to the outsider, he or she will continue to have strange thoughts, distorted perceptions and paranoid ideas. You may like to refer back to Chapter 2 at this stage for a discussion of such symptoms.

You may well wonder at strange convictions expressed by the patient. For example, you will certainly misinterpret unexplained hostility unless you allow for the possibility that the patient may still be the victim of paranoid delusions. No amount of care and support will suffice if he or she believes that the family is hostile. Voices may be heard (and continue to be heard over a very long period) that condemn the sufferer and seem to belong to loved ones.

It seems very clear to me that no family is going to overcome these sort of obstacles, unless the patient can be persuaded they are not for real. Some professionals are shocked at the intensity of feelings of hatred expressed by some patients about their families. Some are shocked by the hostility expressed by some families about sufferers. The explanation usually lies in the ignorance of all concerned about the phenomenon causing the sufferer to think that those who matter most to him or her are really hostile, despite their two-faced attempts to persuade otherwise.

It really is essential that families should be aware of such dangers. It is no less important that sufferers should be aware that their senses may be playing tricks on them, but it should not be assumed that this knowledge will enable them to dismiss false messages as unreal. This 'skill' is acquired very gradually, often over a very long period of time. A young woman patient has named the method that helped her achieve this skill, 'REALITY TESTING'. This is an ongoing process in which the sufferer actually tests the reality of his or her immediate perceptions. It works like this:

At the stage where the sufferer is becoming well enough to sometimes doubt the content of false messages being received from distorted perceptions, or delusional ideas, the carer(s) enters into a contract with him or her. The contract comprises the following agreement:

1. Every time the sufferer has strange ideas or feelings caused, for example, by the intrusion of strange thoughts or by hearing 'voices', he or she will immediately question the carer(s) as to the authenticity of such ideas.
2. The carer(s) will respond by being completely truthful and will find time there and then to discuss the idea as fully as is necessary to reassure or calm the sufferer at that point.

It may be clear that the contract will only work if the sufferer's courage and honesty is met by a correspondingly responsible attitude in the carer(s). This may be difficult to achieve at all times, but it will be immeasurably more positive and rewarding than the more common pitfalls of either colluding with the sufferer in his or her strange ideas (from fear, embarrassment or the 'anything for a peaceful life' syndrome) or ridiculing or contradicting strange statements. The former in no way helps the sufferer cling to reality and the latter encourages him or her to a firm conviction that the rest of the world is 'out of step', or to carefully keep one's thoughts and ideas to oneself! 'Reality testing' should provide a safe environment in which to relearn about reality and the world known to the sufferer before his or her illness; this can only be achieved by acceptance of the sufferer and by open scrutiny of *unpleasant or frightening ideas* caused by symptoms of the illness. Perhaps this approach can best be illustrated by a case study of the young woman mentioned above, who is now well and following a professional career.

PAT: Pat's most troublesome symptom during her schizophrenic break-down was that of 'hearing' her parents' voices condemning her. For a long time, she was convinced that her adoring father was planning, audibly, each night a way to kill her. The rationalisation for this was that Pat had 'heard' him say that she had done some dreadful damage to her mother's health. The girl's first doubts about these false messages occurred when she realised she could still 'hear' her parents' angry voices when she was miles away from them in hospital. Very gradually, she learned to question her own senses but found her resolve weakened each time the phenomenon recurred. As she became more well, so most of the symptoms waned, but she would still sometimes 'hear' her parents blaspheming about her and this would usually be late evening-time, when psychotic symptoms often return. An intelligent girl, Pat came to marvel that her parents seemed able to speak out loud about her (in a remarkably tactless fashion), without moving their lips! She tentatively shared this puzzling information with them during a more confident phase and, as a result of the insight thus gained by all, it was arranged that the girl would *always* challenge her mother and father if she believed they were talking about her. They, in turn, would *always* encourage this openness and would encourage Pat to talk about her feelings and would yet again remind her that her family did not make a habit of discussing others in a disparaging way.

In practice, over a very long period, many a happy evening of playing cards, chatting, or watching television was ruined for the parents by an anguished '*What* did you say?' from a suddenly distraught daughter. The parents tried not to show their distress, and this was not always possible, but Pat very gradually *learned to distrust her senses rather than her loved ones*. She would go to bed reassured yet again by her relatives' genuine response to her agitated queries, but it seems that the carers often had a disturbed night following the realisation that their apparently well and normal daughter was still being tortured by the symptoms of paranoia.

Pat maintains that this 'reality testing' – later modified to discussion about fleeting fears and worries – was one of the most important factors in helping her to regain good health. She was able to go on and use the lessons learned when symptoms occurred in different surroundings, with people with whom she could not talk confidentially. *She had come to terms with her own frailty.*

It is probably clear that this sort of approach is hard work, wearing and sometimes depressing; it is so much easier to look at an able-bodied, seemingly healthy relative and persuade oneself that all is well. Only those who have the patience and courage to face up to some of the nightmares experienced by victims of this illness will persevere with this approach; it will provide a rare insight into living with schizophrenia and will give a loved one much-needed support.

Not only families can provide 'reality testing' for patients. Some sufferers have little or no contact with their families and then a trusted professional can encourage discussion of doubts and any strange phenomena which may still be occurring. I believe this is more productive than encouraging the sufferer to talk 'positively' about his or her good health – a popular practice! The patient has to learn to survive and this is not likely to be achieved by needing to 'live an act' with everybody. We all need to confide in someone; how much more so the individuals whose very senses let them down.

This type of 'reality testing' can also be achieved in group-work, but at a rather less intesive level. I have found it useful to encourage small groups of recovering and 'recovered' young schizophrenic patients to discuss both their experiences during the acute phase of their illness and any remaining symptoms that puzzle them. It takes some time for this sort of trust to be gained in a group setting, but it is time well spent. It is rewarding to note the looks of profound relief on other faces when a patient mentions lingering suspicions or odd sensations which persist. It is very reassuring to know that you are not alone; if others share the same kind of experiences, then there is a *reason* for them.

There is another advantage to this group-work approach, which brings me to the final point I wish to make on understanding and supporting the patient. Most schizophrenic patients initially find their diagnosis difficult to come to terms with, and this is not surprising considering the attitude of society towards the illness and the stark ugliness of the word in most people's minds. For this reason, many doctors do not attempt to burden their patients with the reality of the diagnosis. I have met patients with no idea that they are schizophrenic and this has not helped them. It is interesting that a lot of work is being carried out looking for explanations as to why some patients suffer relapses, and yet I have seen no mention of the idea that one reason may be the individual's own ignorance of his or her condition. For the sort of reasons we have discussed in detail in this chapter, both patient and relatives need to know the diagnosis and, equally importantly, to understand it. How else can the patient survive? He or she must know that taking medication is essential; that much of his or her perception is likely to be distorted at times; and that feelings of paranoia and messages that others are condemning the sufferer are very probably not based on reality. Without this knowledge, *the patient stands little chance of making and maintaining the relationships that make life bearable*. Finally, the patient who is ignorant of the diagnosis is deprived of the responsibility for his or her own well-being. This is a shame; I find that patients are very anxious to learn everything they can about the illness and the more they learn about it, the more responsible most of them become about their own health and about the health of fellow sufferers. Group-work is a useful tool for enabling patients to talk about the illness and to accept and become quite positive about their handicap.

A DEFINITE STRATEGY

I hope that the reader will not find my recommendations over-simplistic or imagine that I believe them to be easy to carry out. The lives of sufferers and their families are anything but simple, but I do believe it is easier to win through with a definite strategy, rather than having to rely on a piecemeal approach.

9 Stimulation

It is not uncommon to learn of newly diagnosed schizophrenia sufferers idling at home all day, with nothing to take their minds off their illness. It is important that those who care for them should be aware that a structured daily routine is an essential part of the treatment for these patients and, indeed, for all sufferers. Prof Wing comments: '. . . too little stimulation will exacerbate any tendency already present towards social withdrawal, slowness, underactivity and an apparent lack of motivation.'[1]

This is frequently overlooked by professionals, which is not so surprising considering the lack of appropriate resources in many areas. One of the reasons why patients often do well in hospital is that they feel secure (and many mention this) in an environment that is organised and structured. The 'apparent lack of motivation' quoted above is much more a lack of staying power and of 'get up and go'. The patient is largely reliant on others to involve him or her in a programme; once thus involved, there is an incentive to carry on. We all know the lethargic feeling that comes over us once home from work, or whatever, following a satisfying meal and the opportunity to put our feet up for a while. Suddenly, there is little motivation to get up and go out to those evening classes we were so enthusiastic about at the beginning of term! I believe that schizophrenia sufferers are faced with this kind of lethargy much of the time; they have the motivation to start all sorts of things on impulse but rarely are able to maintain this interest and the required energy and determination.

This might indeed be bad news if it were not for the fact that part of the slow recovery from this illness is the gradual return of the lost energy and self-discipline; one of the first signs of this process is the recovery of powers of concentration. It is not surprising that the patient has little interest in pursuing any activity for any length of time when he or she is handicapped by an inability to concentrate on anything at all. Watching a television programme or reading the front page of a newspaper, magazine or book can be mammoth tasks for the recovering schizophrenia sufferer. This only adds to the pain of the illness, as it precludes the usual avenues of escapism used by the rest of us. It also contributes to the frequent complaints of boredom.

A STRUCTURED DAILY PROGRAMME_____

It is not unusual that the patient tends to 'switch off'; unless some sort of stimulating activity is provided, there can be nothing to look forward to other than hours and hours of boredom and, consequently, frustration. Add to this the overwhelming desire for sleep during the day-time hours (as discussed in Chapters 2 and 8), and the typical picture of a patient without a structured programme is sleep throughout the day, punctuated by trips to the kitchen for cups of tea or coffee, and at night-time hours of sitting staring into space or wandering around. This picture will be familiar to many sufferers and their families. It is unlikely to lead to the return of good health and should be avoided right from the start in the interests of all concerned. In contrast, a stimulating, but not too demanding, programme can, and in many cases does, contribute to a return to a more normal way of life. Instead of losing previously acquired skills, the patient relearns these and gradually 'tunes into' an acceptable routine which in turn enables a resumption of normality.

Possibly the biggest obstacle to organising a satisfactory programme for the schizophrenic patient will be the tendency to 'turn the clock' around and to fall asleep at around dawn and be exhausted most of the morning. This is a very real problem, but it does improve with time and in some cases the problem will disappear miraculously with the exclusion of sugar from the diet (see Chapters 10 and 11). Meanwhile, if the patient does not get any sleep for most of the night then he or she will need to sleep on in the morning if they can. This, of course, is only possible if it is workable in practice, which depends on the type of programme available for the patient. Let us take a look at the various possibilities.

DAY CARE RESOURCES_____

These have been discussed in some detail in Chapter 5 and it is in your interests to check (in consultation with the patient) with the professionals concerned what facilities are available in your area.

There is no doubt at all that if the sufferer is not well enough to work or return to college, or whatever, or if there is no work available, then he or she should be offered some day care resource. It is up to you, the family, to push for this if it is not offered. If there is no such facility available in your area, then it is up to you and other families in similar need to bombard your health authority and local authority social services department with demands that these resources be made available. If you are in any doubt as to what is provided in your area and do not feel you are obtaining satisfaction from your enquiries, it may be a good idea to contact your local branch of the National Schizophrenia Fellowship (see the list of useful addresses on page 152) as they should be able to help. It seems, at the time of writing, that nothing will stop the closure of the mental hospitals, so this is the time to insist that some of the money from the sale of the buildings and lands is channelled into appropriate day care facilities. It's up to you if you live in one of those areas where little has been done in the past for the mentally ill. Let us first consider those more fortunate.

If you have been offered a day care resource, this should be ideal so long as it can be used at least three times a week, and preferably each weekday during the initial stages of recovery. The family's role will be to encourage the patient to attend (this will probably be resisted initially) and to help him or her to get up in the morning, if this is a problem.

Socialising

Remember that the patient would rather not make the effort to go out each day, let alone have to mix with other people. This is natural and, although the effort will be worth while, this may not be apparent for some time. Meanwhile, the patient may well complain that the activities are banal, monotonous, childish, etc. All of this may seem to be true, but it is important to remember that the organisers are providing activities for at least some patients who are unable to concentrate effectively and are bereft of any 'staying power'. For these sort of reasons, activities that may seem less than stimulating to the outsider are often pitched at the right level for a patient who has temporarily lost touch with performing even the simplest task or socialising at its most basic.

What I am saying to the family is that it is a mistake to collude with the patient at this stage and to make it easy for him or her to opt out of attending whatever facility has been arranged. What is important is that something is being offered that enables the patient to adapt to a daily routine again. It is interesting that, as good health returns, so the individual will often notice the positive things about the programme, and it is common for the problem of getting the new patient to attend to change to a problem of persuading him or her that the time has come for taking on new challenges. The need to move on can also raise new fears in the family, if the patient is not yet ready to return to work, or if employment is not readily available, as may well be the case in the present climate.

S-G

ALTERNATIVES TO DAY CARE

For those families living in areas where no day care is available for the schizophrenia sufferer, alternatives must be found, and this discussion may well apply to others who have exhausted the available resources and who are not able to work, for whatever reason. Whereas it is a good idea to agitate for reform and to persist with demands for adequate facilities in your district, your immediate energies must be devoted to making sure the patient does not vegetate in the meantime. From the moment he or she is diagnosed and at home during the day, some sort of stimulating activity must be provided. Although there are various alternatives to day care, the latter has the advantage that it is provided in a 'sheltered' environment. The people the patient will meet in such a setting are either professionals or individuals with problems usually caused by illness or handicap. Thus it is rare that too much will be expected of the patient and this is very reassuring to the family as well.

In other settings, the stigma attached to schizophrenia usually means that the sufferer is not protected by a visible or acknowledged handicap which will enable healthy people to make allowances for, and to understand, any apparent failings that may be noticed. This puts pressure on the patient that may be counterproductive and it is probably helpful to confide to someone likely to be responsible and involved with the sufferer at some point in the day that he or she is rather vulnerable following a nervous illness. This extra pressure means that it is likely that the patient will only benefit from short bouts of exposure to any such activity. For example, a college course may be a good idea, but only if it is local, part-time and not too demanding in terms of concentration. Many sufferers have done well on a simple part-time typing course, for example, and they have the reward of knowing that their time is not being wasted; there may well be an end-result to their endeavours apart from their function as a temporary measure to rehabilitate them into a daily routine and mixing with others.

Other possibilities are adult education classes such as pottery, painting, dressmaking or dancing. Many are now run in the day for the benefit of the unemployed and retired sections of the population. Given that the patient has some interest in the subject, or did have previously, then the requirement to attend at a certain place at a certain time a couple of times a week can be very helpful. If the patient can also start to relate to some of the other students, however hesitantly, this will be beneficial as well. Many schizophrenic sufferers are creative and talented in subjects such as art, poetry and music. There may well be opportunities at the local college or schools to join such classes, or amateur orchestras or discussion groups. It need hardly be stated that in the first instance there is little, if any, likelihood that the patient will take the initiative and this area of activity is something into which the family will need to enquire and encourage him or her to take the plunge.

Another possibility is in the field of voluntary work. There are usually openings for this and there may be an opportunity that would suit your patient in the first instance. This may be worth discussing with a social worker at the hospital, or failing that with the Citizens' Advice Bureau or Voluntary Services Co-ordinator in your area. Sometimes there is a little typing that needs doing regularly and this might suit the patient who can type, *as long as it involves going out* to a church, office or whatever to do it. Sometimes, washers-up and tea-makers are very welcome at old age pensioners' clubs, for example. Anything that is not too demanding either intellectually or socially will probably be beneficial at this stage.

Although this cannot always be the answer, I know of cases where an unwell young person has been able to do a few hours' work each day in a business run by a parent. This usually works very well as it is, of course, another form of sheltered environment. Similarly, the patient can certainly be involved in chores around the house *but* only in moderation and only if another member of the family joins in and they do the work together. Where the mother or another member of the family is at home during the day, it may be easier to involve a young person in adult education classes, dancing and the like.

If all else fails, it may be a good idea to get in touch with other families so that your patient has a chance to meet other sufferers. Often, they find things in common (even if it is just the devastating experience of a schizophrenic illness), and may attend a drop-in centre or club together. The National Schizophrenia Fellowship (see useful addresses on page 152) sponsors lots of local groups and there is a good chance that there may be one in your area, or at least a telephone contact, so that you can meet other people involved with the illness. Your patient may well enjoy the group's regular meetings as well, if you can persuade him or her to attend.

THE DAY-TIME PROGRAMME: CONCLUSIONS

To sum up, then, in the first instance you need to enquire about day care facilities, which may include short occupational therapy sessions or supportive group-work sessions. Ideally, your patient should be occupied in this way each weekday to enable a resumption of a normal routine. If these sorts of facilities are not available, you need to do some detective work to sort out any appropriate college courses or adult education classes in which you can engage the patient at least twice a week. Voluntary work may provide some answers, but only if it demands a regular commitment from the sufferer. Make sure you've tapped all the resources in your own home, ranging from the moral support of other family members to the possibility of 'sheltered' employment with family or friends. All these sorts of measure will help in the initial stages, when the patient should not be left to do nothing. If your sufferer has never progressed to the point of being well enough to work and has spent his or her days doing nothing at all for a very long time, I would still advise trying to find some way to encourage him or her to take up some form of activity. I have found that some of these long-term sufferers can be persuaded to join in very informal activities and even group-work once some trust and mutual respect has been achieved. This modest stimulation does have a beneficial effect and it can lead to more involvement.

GOING BACK TO COLLEGE

Before leaving this subject, what about the student whose illness has interrupted a university or college course? Some doctors, but fortunately by no means all, believe that these individuals should be discouraged from pursuing their studies, or even starting them if they have their breakdown before going to college. We do not know what causes schizophrenia, but we have no reason at all to believe that it is hard work or leaving the family home that is to blame. These are popular explanations for the high incidence of breakdown amongst students. In fact, the very age of the average student puts this group in the high-risk area for developing this illness and this is probably the only connection between their studies and schizophrenia. In any event, the student will probably be only too aware if his or her studies incur too much stress and, in this case, is not likely to want to repeat the experience.

What about the other students or potential students (and there are some) whose main frustration lies in the illness having sabotaged all their hard work and unfulfilled ambitions? It is my belief that it is damaging to destroy the hope that one day their studies may be resumed and former potential may be partly fulfilled. Sufferers *can* pick up the threads of their previous lives, including higher education courses, if they can be persuaded that this will not happen quickly in most cases. Much wastage occurs because the young people try to escape from their boredom and remaining symptoms by going back to college too soon, with disastrous results. If they can be encouraged to believe this will be possible, if they still want it, but only when they are really well, then it may well work out this way.

In the meantime, very modest study at a local college or evening class, just to discipline the mind into concentrating on one subject, will be the best preparation for such plans. At least a year or two will probably be needed to demonstrate the ability (hopefully not lost for ever) to apply oneself to a task and to stay with it for as long as is needed. Alongside this, there will be time to learn to cope with any remaining symptoms and to protect oneself from an ever-threatening vulnerability. It is, in my experience, only those sufferers who are able to work at this with quite remarkable patience and faith who do manage to complete their college careers and they, of course, are the lucky ones.

Once again, it is a case of 'give and take' as discussed in the previous, chapter. Any patient who can persuade the family or professionals that he or she can work diligently at becoming well and self-sufficient again surely deserves backing and encouragement to make the effort worth while. Colleges are usually more tolerant than employers about a student's medical history and there are often people at hand to counsel or advise at times of stress. Despite this, I do not believe a sufferer is well enough to go away to college if he or she is not well enough to work.

GOING BACK TO WORK

Unless the patient has a job waiting, then part-time employment is certainly an attractive proposition initially. As long as the work itself is not too mundane for the individual concerned, then several hours a day will probably provide the right amount of stimulation without too much pressure.

Which brings us to another problem facing patients whose recovery, whilst not complete, makes it possible for them to resume working. There is a tendency for both professionals and employers to equate stress with responsibility and the need for initiative. I have seen many schizophrenia sufferers fail in the work situation because they have not been allowed to take on the sort of work which interests them and provides a challenge fitting to their intellectual capacity. Again and again, it seems that sufferers are expected to do assembly-line factory jobs, 'envelope filling' or shelf-stacking work, which may suit some people but can be very frustrating for others. Such work, unless it suits the individual in question, provides no escape from an over-active mind or morbid thoughts. I do not believe that this sort of work protects the sufferer from stress, and if this is all the future seems to offer, regardless of the previous potential of the patient, then it is understandable that he or she often backs out of the work situation, and deteriorates further.

I would say to the family and any professionals involved with the patient's future plans, if he or she has aspirations based on reality (as against wishing to take piano lessons in order to become a concert pianist!) and is prepared to strive for these with patience and tenacity as discussed earlier in this chapter, then do what you can to help these materialise. You may find you are pleasantly surprised in the long term and, in any event, any sustained effort on the part of the sufferer should be a real bonus health-wise.

A note of caution, though, which sadly has nothing whatsoever to do with the patient's ability to cope with responsibility; pensionable jobs will be far harder to obtain than those without a pension scheme backing them. Medical personnel are employed just to protect such schemes and many will discard out of hand any application from a candidate with a diagnosis (however remotely distant) of schizophrenia, regardless of performance before or after the illness. The argument goes that it is foolish to employ staff who may have further breakdowns and thus be a burden on the pension funds. However, even medical personnel are unable to forecast mental illness, so the irony is that the candidate who is accepted for the post may break down weeks, months or years later, whilst the well-controlled schizophrenia sufferer may remain well, provided he or she is allowed to live a normal life.

I believe that some sufferers do relapse because of frustration over the work situation; the recent Community Programme run by the Manpower Services Commission has enabled many sufferers to obtain work (albeit usually only for twelve months, because of the rules), and this has often been interesting work. It has been my happy experience that some of them have surprised their employers, and themselves, and have become well-respected members of a work team. Several have been offered more permanent, responsible posts and, not surprisingly, their general functioning and self-confidence have improved correspondingly.

This, then, is what schizophrenia sufferers can do if they are not handicapped by a health record which is no fault of theirs. It is interesting, in this context, that ex-criminals are protected from this sort of discrimination; they do not have to declare their record five years after the event; not so the individual with a history (however brief) of mental illness. It is high time that this sort of anomaly is dealt with if there is to be any 'life after mental illness'[2] for many schizophrenia patients. As it is, those who eventually fulfil their former potential are the lucky ones. They usually have to strive much harder for any opportunity which presents itself and may have had to gain entry to a longed-for career through the back door. In any event, they will almost certainly have to prove themselves over and over again to allay the fears of anyone who is prepared to give them responsible and challenging work. Others will not be so fortunate and it is little wonder that recovered sufferers become lethargic or frustrated about work that offers them neither stimulation nor an escape from an over-active mind. Surely there are enough obstacles on the road to recovery already without people who have had a schizophrenic illness being deprived of opportunities which most of us take for granted?

SPORTS AND EXERCISE

It is well-recorded that many schizophrenia sufferers have considerable creative talent but I have not read anywhere that they often have well above average athletic and sporting skills, although it has been my experience that this is the case. Amongst those I have worked with during the past few years is a young woman who used to run for her county, another who was equally skilled at squash and a third who was on the point of becoming county junior snooker champion at the time he fell ill. Another played golf at fifteen years of age with club professionals! Of the other young people that I know, several were very keen athletes before their illness, and for others their favourite hobbies were team games or swimming. This phenomenon has interested me for some time and it does seem to suggest that some individuals who have a predisposition to contract a schizophrenic illness may also have particularly fine co-ordination in good health! For such sufferers, it can be very frustrating to find themselves tiring after even minimum exertion, and there is a danger that they will push themselves too hard trying to recover their lost potential. On the other hand, others become so discouraged that they give up the previously enjoyed activity completely.

It is almost certainly worthwhile trying to find a middle course and persevering with short bouts of the activity, but only if the individual will not find this too frustrating. For example, the young woman who could previously run long distances has now to content herself with gentle training sessions and shorter runs, as her one (successful) attempt at a marathon since she became ill resulted in immediate relapse. Later she reported, 'I knew I was becoming psychotic throughout the last three miles'. Clearly this feat drained her physical resources and she recognised it while it was happening to her. She has now taken up one of the martial arts and also takes part regularly in other less exhausting athletic activities.

For those individuals who are still recovering from a breakdown, it is particularly helpful, then, if they can have the opportunity to take up physical activities they have enjoyed in the past. This is only likely to occur if relatives or friends make themselves available and persuade the sufferer to join them for a game of some sort, or a swim, perhaps.

Mild exertion, initially for quite short periods, can usually be seen to have a beneficial effect both physically and mentally. One obvious advantage is that this should help control any unwanted weight gain. Unfortunately, the lethargy that is the core of the illness breeds inactivity, escalating any tendency to put on weight with neuroleptic medication, which in turn breeds further inactivity! Most of us feel and look healthier after a bout of enjoyable physical activity, however modest, and research suggests that exercise can be helpful in mental illness.[3,4] Even those sufferers who have never been keen on sport tend to enjoy walking or cycling. Once again, relatives or friends can join in and encourage such activities; so often the sufferer will be loathe to make the first move as the effort needed can seem so enormous, but can be 'jollied' along by the company of others who are trusted and valued. It is important that he or she should enjoy the experience, otherwise there will be little incentive to make the effort a second time! Ideally, a little exercise that is invigorating rather than exhausting should be taken each day.

SUMMING UP

As we have seen, stimulation is an essential part of the sufferer's recovery, and one that is frequently overlooked even by professionals. Until well on the road to recovery, the individual faces an overwhelming temptation – almost a compulsion, in fact – to do nothing, and, at worst, to sleep all day. Even a superficial observation of any sufferer who is left to do just that will confirm that this is very detrimental in this illness, with the lethargy seeming to engulf the individual, who becomes more and more withdrawn and introspective. Whilst it is likely that a newly diagnosed patient will not be interested in partaking of any sort of exercise except, perhaps, for aimless walking, it is important to try and break through that barrier as soon as possible. What is required is a structured programme that provides a fine balance of stimulating activities, including light exercise, together with the opportunity for frequent short breaks in between.

In the past three chapters we have looked at some of the main factors which contribute to the sort of recovery *that can be maintained*, and which maximise on quality of life for the sufferer. In the next, we will discuss in some detail the importance of a sensible diet for people with a schizophrenic illness.

PART III
A Nutritional
Approach

10 Diet and Schizophrenia

Now is a very favourable time for persuading patients and their families that diet can be very important in the treatment of schizophrenia, as it is in the treatment of many other illnesses. There is a sudden, rapidly growing appreciation of the importance of the food we eat in the maintaining of good health. During the past fifty years or so, we have lost sight of this and doctors have become used to the idea that medicine is all-important and, indeed, many patients have become used to equating treatment with drugs.

Up until very recently, those who emphasised the importance of diet were regarded as 'food faddists' or eccentrics, but we are now seeing what amounts to a revolution, spearheaded by members of the public rather than health professionals. Interest has been raised by the tireless efforts of pressure groups such as the Hyperactive Children's Support Group and a handful of nutritionists and nutritionally minded doctors. Books like *E for Additives*[1] and *The Food Scandal*[2] have had phenomenal sales and this demonstrates the public's new determination to learn about the food we eat. The latter publication is to be recommended to anyone interested in the poor nutritional value of the foodstuffs we buy in our shops.

It also explains the findings of the NACNE[3] report, which was commissioned by the Department of Health & Social Security and then withheld from publication for two and a half years until its existence was broadcast by the *Sunday Times* in July 1983. The NACNE report discourages the eating of fats and sugars in the quantities previously common in this country; it encourages us to eat far more vegetables, fruit and wholegrain cereals. In view of the similarity of these recommendations to those given to victims of some of the major diseases, it is disturbing that those intent on protecting their vested interests can 'smother' such a message for so long. The public have reached the sad conclusion that their interests will not be protected unless they demand this; only then will economic interests be put aside. Happily, this is beginning to happen.

The recommendations which will be made about diet in the following pages apply to everyone, not just to schizophrenia sufferers; everyone stands to gain by moving away from our popular junk food diet made up of modern convenience foods. Nevertheless, it seems very probable that such a move has a special significance for schizophrenic patients. It may be that the most startling thing you have observed in your schizophrenic relative is a preoccupation with stodgy food, combined with a ravenous hunger that seems quite insatiable. If this is the case, you may well have noticed, with some distress, a rapid deterioration in table manners. Lastly, the sufferer probably makes tea or coffee almost incessantly between meals (and keeps pace with endless cigarettes, if a tobacco smoker).

THE ROLE OF FOODS:
REFINED CARBOHYDRATES_____

Not all sufferers exhibit such symptoms, but many do; so many that my first suspicions about the role of food in this illness were provoked by constant observation of this phenomenon. However sensible the patient's original diet, there is usually a steady drift towards junk foods and the constant use of stimulants, such as caffeine and tobacco.

Clearly, schizophrenia sufferers are by no means the only section of the population addicted to stimulants and convenience foods. It is the *extent* of the addiction in these patients that is remarkable. The sort of foods typically involved are white bread and rolls, cakes, pastries, chocolates, hamburgers, etc. Many sufferers are just not interested in eating anything other than these refined-carbohydrate foods; they can be very selective indeed in their pursuit of empty calories! What is the underlying mechanism that causes this preoccupation with such foods, together with a ravenous hunger?

Let us look at just one possibility: serotonin production. This neurotransmitter, which is affected by neuroleptic drugs, can be derived from tryptophan, which is contained in protein in our diet. Prof Wurtman and his colleagues at the Massachusetts Institute of Technology have carried out interesting work on the conversion of tryptophan into serotonin; they find that it is 'influenced by the proportion of carbo-hydrate in the diet; the synthesis of serotonin in turn affects the proportion of carbohydrate an individual subsequently chooses to eat.'[4] These researchers further comment: 'the release of serotonin . . . delivers signals to widely scattered groups of neurons that control such things as sleep, mood and appetite.'[5]

Thus, it seems that the food we eat and the quantity and timing of this intake can directly influence our brain functioning. The above work suggests that there is a sophisticated 'feedback' system by which our choice of food – ie protein or carbohydrate – is determined by the contents of previous meals, so that a desirable balance is maintained. Presumably, this system operates properly only in ideal conditions; it appears not to be working efficiently in those schizophrenic patients who seek out refined carbohydrates all the time, and with a constantly avid appetite. This amounts to an overwhelming compulsion and one young woman explained recently: 'As I sit down to eat my meal, I pray I shall be able to eat it in a restrained manner, instead of wolfing it down.' She shuddered and muttered that as a rule this was a vain hope. This is a young woman who normally has an excellent diet and leads an active life, but during her two acute breakdowns (the second occurred because she had not understood the need to continue to take medication) she has demonstrated the eating pattern we are discussing. More unusually, she is also very much aware of this compulsion to devour the food like a starving animal. She has noticed, without prompting, that foods containing wheat are the main culprits for her.

It is interesting to consider that serotonin is known to have a tranquillising effect; that is, if a sufficient quantity is available, it can induce sleep. It seems likely that some patients' eating habits may produce surplus serotonin and some neuroleptic drug treatments tend to check this. Certainly, I have found that the exclusion of sugars and refined starches from a sufferer's diet can result in the 'magical' disappearance of much of the lethargy and sleepiness experienced previously, particularly in the mornings. Conversely, it is possible to observe the detrimental effects of continuous bingeing of these foods during the day; the individual becomes more and more 'pasty', and puffy around the lower half of the face, and increasingly lethargic and exhausted. The immediate 'uplift' provided by such foods and of stimulants like caffeine is quickly followed by a 'let down' feeling and a craving for yet more of the same.

This brings us to the subject of fluctuating blood sugar levels. The importance of blood sugar levels becomes clear if we realise that the sugar in our blood is an important nutrient for the brain as well as an important energy resource. Many nutritionally minded doctors believe that low blood sugar – hypoglycaemia – is very common in schizophrenia. They refer to this condition as functional hypoglycaemia:

All the sugar and starch we eat is broken down into glucose which enters the bloodstream. Normally, the pancreas then reacts by producing insulin, which takes the glucose out of the blood into the cells. If we constantly eat sugar, the pancreas is constantly stimulated. If we eat any carbohydrate in its refined form (sugar, sweets, chocolate, white flour), digestion is rapid and glucose enters the blood in a violent rush.[6]

This can lead to the pancreas over-reacting and producing too much insulin, which in turn results in blood glucose taking an uncomfortable drop, causing further craving for more sugars and starches. It may be that the increasing incidence of functional hypoglycaemia correlates with the dramatic increase in the consumption of sugar. In the nineteenth century, 7lb of sugar per person per year were consumed in Britain; today, the figure is 115lb per person per year.[7] The human body could hardly have adapted to these sort of changes in so short a time! However, Philpott points out that abnormal sugar levels 'can be caused by any substance to which the person reacts maladaptively. The simple fact of the matter is that abnormal sugar levels in the body are caused by allergic-like reactions to specific substances.'[8]

Although refined carbohydrates are usually the cause of functional hypoglycaemia, it should also be remembered that any substance to which the individual is allergic may also be to blame. For this reason, it is important to eliminate such offending substances in the first instance; Chapter 11 is devoted to this subject. Having looked at Chapter 11 in some detail, the reader will realise that allergy may well explain the schizophrenia sufferer's 'bingeing' of stodgy foods, and, indeed, of any foods. I would suggest, therefore, that the suggestions made in Chapter 11 should be applied within the broader context of the present discussion on diet and schizophrenia.

ALL ABOUT THE DIET

The first requirement of a good diet is that it should be nutritious. This may seem an obvious comment, but it is one that has escaped the attention of many of us over a long period. This is not the place for a detailed discussion about the nutritional content of various foods, but excellent coverage can be found in books such as *Vitamin Vitality*[9] and *The Whole Health Manual*.[10] Patrick Holford, the author of these books, refers to a 'vitality diet'. This is the sort of diet which puts emphasis on high fibre and nutritious foods such as wholegrains, raw fruits and vegetables, nuts and seeds, and beans and lentils, cuts down on fats and sugars, and omits all processed foods. I feel his name for such a diet has a message for anyone involved in the seemingly devitalising process of this illness. It is my belief that some of this process is the result of the sort of eating habits we have been discussing. For this reason, I want to interest patients, their families, and involved health professionals, in measures to combat and, perhaps, reverse this process.

The diet discussed below is aimed at restricting sugars to those occurring naturally in the complex carbohydrates such as fruits, vegetables and wholegrains. Our bodies have been designed to cope with these slow-releasing sugars, but are ill-equipped to handle the sugars contained in the refined carbohydrates which have become the mainstay of so many people's diets.

Foods to be Avoided
Chocolate and other sweets
All sugars, including honey, and the various artificial sweeteners
White flour and white rice
All processed breakfast cereals
Cakes, biscuits and pastries
White bread and rolls
Large quantities of dried fruits
Large quantities of citrus fruits
Processed meats, which contain added sugar
Tinned foods, which contain added sugar (look at the label)
Caffeine-containing drinks such as coffee, colas and strong tea
All alcoholic drinks (heavy in sugar)
Icecream

Foods to be Encouraged
Wholegrain rice (ie brown rice, with its delicious nutty taste)
Potatoes, preferably with their skins, well scrubbed, as in baked jacket potatoes
Wholemeal bread – up to 3 slices per day
Muesli, adding your own fruit and nuts – look on the label and avoid brands with added sugar
Nuts of all kinds, as fresh as possible
Dried fruits, in moderation
Fresh fruits – several helpings per day
Vegetables of all kinds – at least several helpings per day, raw or cooked until just tender, but still crunchy
Seeds, such as sesame, sunflower or pumpkin – add to muesli or yoghurts, or use as snacks

Yoghurts, the natural live type if possible. Add fruit, nuts, muesli or unsweetened jams to provide extra flavour

Plenty of protein such as:

Eggs, boiled or poached (no more than seven per week)

Cheese (ideally low-fat kinds)

Meats, particularly liver, kidneys and poultry

Fish of all kinds, including tinned in oil. Fresh herrings, mackerel or trout are particularly good

Lentils and beans in a 1:2 ratio with wholegrain rice

Herbal teas – fruit teas such as rosehip or mixed fruit are sweet and tasty

Coffee substitutes such as dandelion coffee or chicory. As a last resort, decaffeinated coffee may be used sparingly, or very weak tea

Unsweetened fruit juices may be used, but only if diluted in equal parts with water or mineral water – two glasses per day

Chapter 11 should be read carefully before any decision is made to include wheat or other gluten-containing cereals in the diet in the first instance. Alternatives to bread are suggested and muesli can be made with seeds, nuts, dried fruit and fresh fruit, with or without wholegrain rice or millet as well. This can be soaked in a little fruit juice overnight and eaten with milk, cream, yoghurt or fruit juice next morning.

Tips for Following the Diet

Hopefully, after any initial shock, it is now evident that there is plenty of variety available in the above suggestions. The diet may constitute a dramatic change in lifestyle, but is not over-restrictive.

An important principle is to avoid feeling hungry; this can be achieved by eating frequent small meals, or by eating three main meals (not too heavy) with a snack between each meal and during the evening. Foods that are useful for snacks are fruits (bananas are filling), nuts and seeds, and vegetables such as raw carrots or celery, or baked jacket potatoes. Puffed rice cakes are available from most health food shops and they make a useful and nourishing snack (low in calories), lightly toasted with, say, Marmite, cheese or one of the new 'jams' that have no added sugar.

Eating breakfast is a *must* and this can consist of eggs (boiled or poached) with wholemeal toast, puffed rice cakes or bacon. Other cooked breakfast dishes can be made up of mushrooms, tomatoes, baked beans, etc. Alternatively, muesli or yoghurt makes a substantial breakfast, both with a helping of fresh fruit.

Lunch can be based on a large salad, which can be made up of a selection including just about every vegetable that can be eaten raw – for example, crisp lettuce, Chinese leaves, shredded white cabbage, carrot, cress, cucumber, celery, green and red peppers, spring onions, radishes, chicory, fennel, tomatoes, beetroot, etc. In particular, bean sprouts are delicious and especially rich in nutrients; a superb selection can be bought in a carton in larger branches of a well-known health food store, or you can grow your own. (Mung beans and alfalfa are the easiest to grow. Put the beans in a jar and cover them with water, leave to soak overnight. Next day, pour off the excess water and place the beans in a jar, covering the top with a piece of muslin. Stand the jar on a window-sill. Rinse and drain twice a day until the seeds sprout; then leave them uncovered for a few hours, after which they should be ready to eat. Refrigerate those not eaten; they will last for several days this way. Alternatively, you can buy 'bean sprouters' from most health food stores.)

Ring the changes with your salads by adding nuts, seeds or chopped fruit. The book *Raw Energy*[11] gives plenty of ways to make such dishes really appetising. Add whatever protein you fancy to this lunch dish – egg, cheese, meat or fish.

The evening meal can be based on a rice dish (brown, of course!), or a jacket potato, with a couple of cooked vegetables or a side salad. Add whatever protein appeals to you. For ideas on dishes containing beans and lentils, and delicious nut 'roasts', *The Cranks Recipe Book*[12] is recommended.

RECIPES

Meanwhile, here are some well tried and tested recipes that are suitable for this diet. Many commonly cooked dishes are not included – though they are quite acceptable for this purpose – as any cookery book will contain a variety of such recipes.

The quantities suggested are appropriate for four persons – the amounts can be adjusted as necessary.

FRIED RICE

1 medium-sized onion
8oz (250g) brown rice
a little oil for frying
water (as specified on rice packet) or same amount of stock
1 stock cube or 1 teaspoon Marmite
2 free-range eggs, lightly beaten

Chop up the onion and fry it with the rice in the oil, turning the mixture occasionally, for about 5 minutes. Heat the water or stock and dissolve the stock cube or Marmite in it. Add it to the rice and onion, bring to the boil, then lower the heat and simmer until all the liquid is absorbed (about 40 minutes). Still on the heat, make a hole in the middle of the rice and add the eggs. Stir the eggs gently into the rice. If desired, chopped-up cooked chicken or turkey can be added to this dish when the liquid is poured in. Alternatively, add bean sprouts, mushrooms or chopped cooked bacon.

SAVOURY RICE

Water (as specified on rice packet) or same amount of stock
8oz (250g) brown rice
1 tablespoon wine vinegar or French dressing
1 green pepper, deseeded and chopped
1 red pepper, deseeded and chopped or 2 tomatoes, deseeded and chopped
a handful of cashew nuts, hazelnuts or peanuts
a handful of sultanas

Bring the liquid to the boil, and add the rice. Bring it back to boil, then turn down the heat and simmer with the lid on until all the water has been absorbed (about 40 minutes). Add the vinegar or dressing while the rice is still hot. Add the chopped peppers/tomatoes and the other ingredients when the rice has cooled.

This makes an appetising addition to salads, and keeps well in the refrigerator.

STIR-FRY VEGETABLES

1 green pepper, deseeded
3 or 4 sticks celery
beansprouts, green cabbage, cauliflower, etc, as required
a little oil for frying
soy sauce (optional)
sesame seed oil (optional)

Cut the celery and green pepper into thin slices. Shred or cut the other vegetables, breaking the cauliflower into small florets. Heat a little oil in wok or frying-pan and cook first those vegetables needing more time, such as cabbage and cauliflower. Add the pepper and celery for the last 5 minutes, sprinkling with soy sauce or sesame seed oil, if liked. Serve immediately.

The secret is to 'stir' (turn) the vegetables all the time, cooking until just tender but still crunchy, on a fast heat – this way you do not lose too many nutrients.

STIR-FRY MUSHROOMS

Leave the mushrooms whole, complete with peel and stalks. Wipe them clean and stir-fry in a little hot fat until they are just softening.

STIR-FRY TOMATOES

Rinse and quarter the tomatoes, and cook them as for mushrooms. The tomatoes will be ready in a much shorter time.

STIR-FRY CHICKEN OR TURKEY

Cut the meat into slivers (about 3oz (90g) per person will be plenty as the meat goes further this way). Stir-fry the slivers in hot fat until the meat turns white. Sprinkle with soy sauce or sesame seed oil. Add some chopped green pepper and/or sliced celery and/or chopped spring onions, turning the food over all the while. After a few minutes, add almonds or cashew nuts, if liked, and serve immediately.

STIR-FRY BEEF

Use cheap frying steak and slice very thinly, *against the grain*. Stir-fry in hot oil until the meat is tender and sprinkle with soy sauce or sesame seed oil. Add stir-fried mushrooms or stir-fried tomato quarters and after a couple of minutes the dish will be ready for serving.

MEAT TIKKA

Cut 1lb (450g) chicken or lamb into cubes and leave in a mixture made up of 1 small carton natural, live yoghurt and 2 teaspoons curry powder, well mixed. After a few hours, the meat can be taken out of the 'marinade' and grilled (easiest on skewers) until cooked. It is good with brown rice and a side salad.

CHICKEN WITH PINEAPPLE

4 chicken joints, skinned
1 green pepper, deseeded and chopped
1 small onion, chopped
1 large tin pineapple rings (in natural juice)
2 teaspoons curry powder
1 teaspoon arrowroot

Place the chicken joints in a casserole dish. Cover them with the pepper and onion, and the drained pineapple rings. Mix the pineapple juice, 2 tablespoons water, curry powder and arrowroot together and heat them in a saucepan, stirring all the time. When this mixture has thickened, pour it over the meat, and put in the middle of a moderately heated oven for 1½ hours. Serve with brown rice and green beans or peas.

COLE-SLAW

½ small white cabbage
2 large carrots
1 dessert apple, cored
1 small onion

Grate all the ingredients and mix well together. It is good with a little Cheddar cheese grated and added just before serving. Also, a small quantity of natural yoghurt can be stirred in before serving. Cole-slaw keeps well in a covered container in the refrigerator.

Dieters will probably crave forbidden chocolates and sweets sometimes and recipes such as the following make very welcome substitutes, *occasionally*.

HOBBIT LOG

(Veronica Oxley and Jennifer Pinker)[13]

2½oz (75g) dates, chopped
4oz (125g) dried apricots, chopped
2½oz (75g) sultanas
2½oz (75g) raisins, chopped
1½oz (40g) prunes, chopped
4fl oz (100ml) boiling water
2oz (60g) peanuts, chopped
2 teaspoons lemon juice
1½oz (40g) desiccated coconut
2½oz (75g) sunflower seeds
1½oz (40g) skimmed milk powder
extra 2½oz (75g) desiccated coconut

Place the dried fruits in a bowl. Add the boiling water, and allow to stand for 10 minutes to soften the fruit. Add the peanuts, lemon juice, coconut, sunflower seeds and milk powder. Mix well. Form the mixture into a log 2in (5cm) in diameter. Roll the log in the extra coconut. Refrigerate for a few hours and then cut into 25 even slices.

Try wrapping some individual slices in cling film and adding a slice to packed lunches etc.

There are several delicious recipes for desserts for those attempting a wheat-free diet on page 129–31.

THE HEALTHY DIET: SUMMARY_____

The first important point is that most of us eat much too much salt as well as too much sugar. There is no need to add salt to your cooking and no need to sprinkle it on your food either; try gradually cutting down if this is your usual habit. Although no fish recipes are included above, it is recommended that fresh or tinned oily fish should be eaten at least three times a week, preferably more. It is becoming clear that the oils in such fish are very important and they may well be of special importance in schizophrenia. The traditional fish and chips from the local shop are not acceptable as the batter contains white flour, but fish can be fried at home or, preferably, grilled or baked. As for chips, they are not a particularly nourishing way of preparing potatoes. However, home cooked ones may well be better than mashed potatoes, as, when making the latter, we literally mash out any remaining vitamins!

It is probably clear by now that this diet is as much about eating fresh, wholesome foods as about cutting out convenience foods. Hoffer sums up the basic theme well by stipulating five main criteria for a diet in the treatment of schizophrenia.[14] He says the food should be **whole** (as in wholegrain), **alive** (fresh and raw whenever possible), **varied** (without excessive dependence on any one food), **non-toxic** (and therefore free from additives – he considers sugar to be a toxic additive), and, lastly, **indigenous** (meaning that our food should be from our own environment as much as possible, with less emphasis on imported foods).

Several references have been made to food being **raw** where possible. The authors of the book *Raw Energy* state that a high-raw diet affects blood sugar levels. They say:

It is now widely accepted that functional hypoglycaemia, which is believed to be widespread, is responsible for that mid- to late-afternoon tiredness peak that affects so many people and has them reaching for strong cups of coffee and sweet snacks 'just to keep going' . . . Dr John Douglass and others who recommend a high-raw diet for diabetics do so because raw fibre helps to stabilise blood sugar levels. It does the same for someone suffering from persistently low blood sugar levels, and abolishes the mood swings and other symptoms that characterise hypoglycaemia.[15]

Several references have also been made to food being whole. It is now appreciated by most people that the refining of cereals such as flour and rice robs the foods of important vitamins and minerals. Chromium is a mineral that has an important function in the regulating of blood sugar levels, and 98 per cent of this precious substance is lost in the production of white flour and 92 per cent in the polishing of rice![16] Perhaps this sort of information might serve to persuade the whole family that a diet such as the one recommended would benefit everyone; not just the member of the family who already suffers from a debilitating illness.

The question of expense sometimes worries people. For example, fresh foods such as salads can be relatively scarce in winter-time and more expensive than at other times. Protein can also be expensive. However, all the food you buy will be *nourishment*, which is much more than can be said for most convenience foods, and if you tot up the cost of these, including the inevitable snacks of chocolate, icecreams and biscuits, you may be surprised! For instance, one does not eat the same quantity of high-fibre 'whole' foods as of refined carbohydrates. One piece of wholemeal bread is much more satisfying and filling than a piece of that modern-day wonder, the white sliced loaf.

There has been no mention of fats in this discussion, but I suspect the reader will have realised that the diet cuts back quite dramatically on the amounts usually consumed. Olive oil is recommended for cooking purposes and butter is quite suitable for the modest amount of bread that is allowed, unless, of course there is a temptation to pile it on too thickly.

Allergy has not been discussed in the context of this recommended diet, but any allergens that are discovered must be added to the list of foods to be avoided. As wheat gluten is a relatively common one, this is often restricted but the information and recipes offered in this chapter and the next should make it possible to work out a nourishing and attractive diet.

The good news is that the craving for stodgy, sugary foods fades if the individual gives them up completely, in much the same way that many of us have only been able to give up tobacco when we have finally realised that having the occasional cigarette keeps the addiction alive. It is at the beginning that a lot of support is needed; later, when the sufferer starts to feel less lethargic and 'flat', he or she has more incentive to persevere with the diet. Meanwhile, it really is asking too much of human nature to expect a dieter to resist temptations if forbidden foods are left lying around for the eating.

Everyone stands to gain by moving towards the sort of diet suggested; it is much healthier than the modern convenience foods we have grown used to in western societies, so the whole household should benefit by the change. Any attempts to change the diet of a sufferer in your family will certainly stand more chance if he or she is not made to feel a food freak. Finally, do be patient; considerable effort will be required by everyone concerned, and there will be occasions when the patient seems to sabotage all your hard work. Don't give up at the first setback; it won't be the last, because we are all only human. Eating patterns *can* be changed and there is everything to be gained by persevering. Not least will be the control of the unwanted weight-gain experienced by so many individuals on neuroleptic medication. In the next chapter we will look at the possible role played by allergy and other forms of food intolerance in the process of this disease.

11 Allergy and Other Forms of Food Intolerance

Allergy is a word that means different things to different people. To the layperson, it is simply a term used to describe an individual's inability to tolerate a food, chemical or pollen. For doctors, the subject has been one of hot debate during most of this century. Until very recently, the orthodox medical view has been that allergy is concerned only with an abnormal immune response. This has meant that unless the patient could fit into the required slot and produce the appropriate antibodies in laboratory testing, it was another case of 'It's all in the mind.' The man who invented the term 'allergy', back in 1906, a Frenchman called Clemens Von Pirquet, did not share this narrow approach to the subject. It seems he commented on conditions that produce 'supersensitivity' rather than 'immunity', saying that the two can be 'most closely related'.[1]

It has taken nearly eight decades for the medical profession to catch up with this viewpoint, and the reader may like to refer to a report published in 1984 called *Food Intolerance and Food Aversion*. This document groups all the different mechanisms, including some as yet unidentified, that cause an adverse reaction to any food in any one person, under the heading of 'food intolerance'. Food allergy is described as 'a form of food intolerance in which there is also evidence of an abnormal immuno-logical reaction to the food'.[2] To avoid further confusion, I have chosen a heading for this present chapter that incorporates this definition.

As might be expected, now that the subject is becoming 'respectable', evidence is pouring in to support the teachings of the clinical ecologists and allergists who have treated patients for all sorts of food intolerance for so many years. Much exciting research is now taking place to prove the sort of thing that Hippocrates, the father of medicine, observed in his lifetime; that particular foods or changes in diet make some individuals ill.

Although the discipline of psychiatry can scarcely be happy with the limited number of tools at hand with which to treat schizophrenia, careful research stretching back over thirty years demonstrating a connection between diet and this illness has been persistently ignored up until the present time. What a shame, when a dietary approach of this nature is harmless and potentially beneficial to at least some sufferers. Even the most uninterested psychiatrist is bound to admit to an enquiring patient that 'It can't do you any harm.' This is all some psychiatrists do say – a sadly inadequate response in the face of the apathy at the core of the illness, coupled with the patient's probable craving for flour-containing foods (see Chapter 10 for a detailed discussion on this point). However, a handful of psychiatrists are prepared to encourage their patients to try a dietary approach and I have been fortunate enough to have had the opportunity to work with several such open-minded doctors.

A worrying aspect of this 'it's not yet proven' attitude is that there seems to be an over-dependence on 'double-blind' controlled research – that is, research in which neither the researchers nor the participants know who is receiving the 'treatment' and who is receiving a placebo – instead of the use of initiative and the recognition of each patient's individuality. Even if the patient does have a recognisable illness, surely no doctor would suggest that there is only *one* schizophrenia. In view of the fact that we do not yet understand the various subdivisions of the illness, we may wait a very long time for a remedy universal to all sufferers.

Meanwhile, there is no sign at the time of writing of any change within NHS hospitals; on arrival there, the patient is bombarded with stodgy foods containing refined flour and sugar. Between meals, there is the hospital shop and patients' canteen, selling more of the same and, of course, the inevitable chocolate. Before going any further, it might be useful at this stage to take a closer look at some of the research which indicates that a dietary approach could be an important factor in the treatment of schizophrenia.

In 1953, Dr Lauretta Bender drew attention to her observations that there is an unusual incidence of coeliac disease among schizophrenic children.[3] Thirteen years later, she had recorded twenty cases among two thousand cases of schizophrenia; this figure is much higher than could be expected within an average population of the same size. In 1961, Graff and Handford reported that four out of thirty-seven schizophrenic male patients admitted to one hospital unit in one year had a history of coeliac disease in childhood.[4]

F. C. Dohan, an American psychiatrist, became interested in these observations. Coeliac disease responds only to the elimination from the diet of gluten, a protein contained in wheat and other cereal grains. The condition not only causes 'gut' problems, with crippling diarrhoea, but is known to provoke behaviour disturbance and psychological problems which, at their most acute, can resemble psychosis. Most patients regain good health if they do not eat foods containing gluten, but some need to avoid milk as well. Dohan wondered whether some individuals have an inherited susceptibility to both coeliac disease and schizophrenia. He studied the incidence of the latter illness in different grain-eating societies throughout the world. He found that, although schizophrenia exists in all societies, the incidence is less in areas where the main crops for consumption are cereals other than wheat or rye, and least of all where foods such as millet, maize and sweet potatoes replace the more common cereals. Not only is the incidence of schizophrenia less, but the course of the illness also seems to be more benign.[5]

Dohan went on to study the incidence of first admissions to hospital for patients with a diagnosis of schizophrenia during World War II, when some countries suffered an acute shortage of cereal grains. He found that such admissions dropped significantly in those countries, although hospital facilities were adequate and admissions for other forms of psychoses actually increased. The decrease in admissions for schizophrenia coincided with shortages of wheat in particular, and, to a lesser extent, shortages of rye.[6]

All of the above information led Dohan to conclude that wheat and rye are implicated in the development and course of schizophrenia but that other cereals are probably involved to a lesser extent. In a letter to the Editor of *The Lancet*, this researcher comments: '. . . coeliac disease and schizophrenia may be genetically related – a proposition which deserves formal testing by careful family studies of proven coeliacs.'[7] It seems more likely that this theory will be explored by studying families of 'proven' schizophrenics, as the Schizophrenia Association of Great Britain is about to sponsor such research at Addenbrooke's Hospital in Cambridge.

Meanwhile, in 1969, Dohan, Grasberger and colleagues conducted a study among male patients in a locked psychiatric ward.[8] Admission to such a ward follows a worsening of the condition, so release to an open ward (with full privileges) provides a reliable indication of improvement in symptoms. Those patients randomly assigned to a diet free of cereals and milk (as some coeliac patients do not improve until milk is removed from the diet) were released to an open ward 'considerably more rapidly' than those on a high cereal diet. When, unknown to the staff, wheat gluten was added to the diet of the former group, the differences were cancelled out. Meanwhile, there was no correlation between the progress of non-schizophrenic patients and their diets.

In 1976, Singh and Kay reported work that supported these findings.[9] They removed all cereal grain and milk from the diet of fourteen patients over a period of as many weeks. A drink containing wheat gluten was given for seven weeks or so, and a drink containing soy protein for the rest of the time. Neither patients nor those assessing them knew the content of the drinks and they were given to different patients at different times. Patients continued to receive their usual medication throughout and the researchers concluded that the results 'showed that wheat gluten had the effect of exacerbating the schizophrenic process and diminishing response to treatment'.

I suspect that the medical profession as a whole has missed the message contained in this research; which is that the omission of certain foods from the diet serves as a potential treatment which is *complementary* to medication. Many doctors worry about the dangers of drug treatment; they should surely be anxious to try any harmless means of improving its efficiency. Such measures can have a twofold benefit – the patient's well-being, while on drug treatment, may be improved, and the quantities of medication required may be reduced. The Brain Bio Centre in Princeton, USA, believes that 4 per cent of all hospitalised schizophrenic patients are sensitive to wheat gluten, and around 10 per cent of all those out in the community.[10] They, not unreasonably, recommend that all patients diagnosed as schizophrenic should try omitting this substance from their diets.

Meanwhile, my own experience with patients living in the community leads me to suspect that a greater proportion than 10 per cent will gain from omitting wheat from their diets. The earlier discussion on the title of this chapter indicated that there are various mechanisms underlying food intolerance and it seems that there may be other factors to be considered as well as an innate sensitivity to certain grains and, perhaps, milk. Research done by Hemmings[11] suggests that milk and wheat proteins are not broken down completely before entering the bloodstream and that these molecules can be traced to the brain. Zioudrou, Streaty and Klee have demonstrated that opioid peptides are derived from wheat and milk proteins in the course of digestion and that these have similar properties to the naturally occurring molecules called endorphins, which affect the functioning of the brain, acting as hormones and neurotransmitters. These dietary peptides are called exorphins because of 'their exogenous origin and morphine-like activity'.[12]

Also present in pepsin digests of wheat gluten, according to these researchers, are substances which have a stimulatory action rather than a sedating one. Thus, we come back to the direct effect on brain functioning of the food we eat (refer back to Chapter 10 for a detailed discussion on this subject). Once again, I would draw the reader's attention to the obvious craving many sufferers have for wheat products! There are also a few who drink milk by the bottle, rather than the glass – it may well be clear by now that this is unlikely to be good for them.

What other foods seem to be implicated in this illness? We have already discussed sugar in the last chapter and there has been passing mention of chocolate. Many sufferers (and not just sufferers!) are clearly addicted to this latter substance and it may be that the presence of phenylethylamine, with its possible hallucinatory effect, may be a factor in aggravating the symptoms of schizophrenia. Vicky Rippere, discussing the frequency with which certain foods caused problems amongst those taking part in her survey on allergy, comments: 'The high proportion of people mentioning chocolate and sugar is consistent with findings about anomalies of carbohydrate metabolism in various forms of mental illness, including schizophrenia.'[13]

Other common offenders are stimulants such as caffeine and tobacco. Once again, where a food is craved or appears again and again on the individual's choice of menu, beware! The mechanism at work here is described by clinical ecologists as 'masked allergy'. They believe that the offending food upsets the body's mechanism; the individual does not connect that food with any symptoms which follow (unless it is so rarely consumed that the tie-up is obvious and the food is then avoided) and continues to eat it; so the body learns to 'maladapt' to the offending substance, at which point the individual experiences worse symptoms in its absence. Such is the stuff of addiction! By omitting the food entirely from the diet (withdrawal symptoms are to be expected) for a certain minimal period, it can then be tried again, to test for adverse reactions. This is the reason for using elimination diets to identify the offending foods in individuals suspected of food intolerance.

Although there are various laboratory tests available for the detection of allergies, these are not yet completely reliable when it comes to food testing and they can be very expensive and time-consuming. Although much effort and co-operation is required from the patient and, hopefully, careful monitoring and support from the practitioner, the use of exclusion diets is favoured by most clinical ecologists. As interest in the subject grows, other members of the medical profession are beginning to use this approach to food intolerance as well.[14] Certain conditions seem to be linked with certain foods and, as this is becoming recognised, so it is less tedious searching for offending substances. Thus, we can now consider foods such as chocolate, red wine, cheese and oranges first, if we suffer from migraine headaches and suspect food allergy to be the cause. Similarly, we can consider wheat and other gluten-containing cereals, chocolate, sugar and milk in the first instance when looking for food intolerance in schizophrenia.

How do we go about tackling this sort of approach? Firstly, it may now be clear that the recommendation in Chapter 10 is to cut right down on the consumption of sugar, chocolate, all refined flours and white rice. Even if the sufferer is not affected by wheat, it is preferable that he or she only eats wholegrains, but I would recommend that *all wheat* should be omitted from the diet in the first instance and that any other gluten-containing cereals (ie rye, barley and, possibly, oats) should be avoided as much as possible and certainly only eaten in small quantities – no more than once weekly. If there is no improvement within a period of two months, then it may be worth cutting out milk as well for a further month. At the end of this period, and if no improvement has been observed, it is probably worth reintroducing these foods *in moderation only.*

Meanwhile, let us look at ways of achieving a wheat-gluten-free diet without feeling too deprived. Here are some basic rules:

1. Remember that planning for such a diet takes considerable effort on the part of the cook and housekeeper. Allow a week or so to organise the kitchen in such a way that there is always plenty to eat and the menu does not become too monotonous. It will seem easier after the first couple of weeks.

2. At the risk of becoming repetitive, I would remind the reader once again that it is not reasonable to expect a dieter to avoid forbidden foods if these are left lying around for the eating. Try and have available some snacks which are permissible and likely to take the sufferer's mind off craved foods that are *not* permissible in the diet. The craving will wear off eventually.

3. Now for stocking your larder: look at all labels and avoid products which include items such as wheat, starch, modified starch, rusk, cereal and monosodium glutamate (MSG), which is often derived from wheat gluten.

4. Avoid all bread, biscuits, cakes and pastry, except those included in the recipes provided below.

5. Check all so-called 'gluten-free' products for any remaining wheat starch. In particular, most 'gluten-free' breads, bread mixes and flours are not suitable, because of remaining traces of gluten and the

presence of wheat starch. Jubilee and Trufree products are suitable, and are available from Boots and other chemists, as they are supplied on prescription to coeliacs. Unfortunately, these items are expensive and it may be a good idea to forget about bread entirely – see item 6 – if you can.

6. Good substitutes for bread are puffed rice cakes, available from most health food stores; these are a very low calorie product made from wholegrain rice and delicious when lightly toasted.

7. Avoid all beer, spirits and instant coffees unless you can confirm there is no cereal in such products. Beware, cereals are used as fillers in many unexpected products, including toothpaste!

8. Avoid all processed meats, including sausages, unless you can confirm there is no cereal in them – Marks & Spencer's top-quality type are acceptable at the time of writing.

9. Have cooked breakfasts whenever possible; potatoes, puffed rice cakes, eggs, bacon, tomatoes, mushrooms, etc, are all very suitable. As a last resort, cornflakes and Rice Krispies can be eaten, but they are not ideal as they are coated in sugar, and not particularly nutritious compared with a cooked breakfast or yoghurt and fruit or muesli (suggestions for a wheat-free version of this dish are given later).

10. For packed lunches, replace bread with jacket potato or puffed rice cakes, or, occasionally, potato crisps (look at the label!). Cold meats, tinned fish, cheese or hard-boiled eggs with salad make good lunches. You can add fresh fruit, dried fruit and nuts or sunflower seeds. Some tinned tomato soups are safe. If not, home-made soups are better still and can be taken in a flask for a warming lunch during the winter.

11. For 'fillers up', look for ideas in 10 above. Add cheese or Marmite to puffed rice cakes, or spread them with the new 'sugar-free' jams. Other treats include carob bars (without added sugar), carob-coated puffed rice cakes and 'Sunflower' bars, all at most health food stores. Also try the Hobbit Log recipe in Chapter 10.

12. Vary the diet as much as possible; for a full discussion on this point, see the end of this chapter.

For several years now I have been supporting sufferers in their efforts to omit wheat and other gluten-containing grains from their diets (increasingly, I am now finding that other ailments respond dramatically to the exclusion of wheat from the diet). The first priority seemed to be the need to find recipes which offered attractive alternatives to the usual wheat-containing ones. This turned out to be easier said than done. There are plenty of books available, containing a seemingly endless choice of such recipes, but this cook found that some of them would put off the most enthusiastic dieter! I persevered and found that about one in every six recipes proved to be a real find; the sort of dish that the whole family would fight over, and this must be a measure of a recipe worth recommending. I make no apologies for offering no original recipes, as I am no recipe book author, let alone a particularly talented cook. However, I can assure the reader that all of the following recipes are well-tried and tested. I am glad to acknowledge the author of each recipe, and further details of the relevant publication, etc, are available under the references listed for this chapter. In some cases, the publications are also recommended under 'Further Reading' at the end of this book.

GLUTEN-FREE RECIPES

The quantities suggested are appropriate for four persons – the amounts can be adjusted as necessary.

MILLET CROQUETTES

(Honor J. Campbell)[15]

8oz (250g) millet flakes
1 pint (600ml) water
1 onion, finely chopped, and fried
parsley or chives
2 eggs, beaten
2–3 tablespoons grated cheese
butter or oil for frying

Combine the millet flakes with the water and simmer gently, stirring continuously until thick. Remove from the heat and leave in the pan until cool. Then mix in the fried onion, parsley or chives, beaten eggs and grated cheese. Shape the mixture into sausages and fry in butter or oil until golden brown.

SAVOURY PASTRY

(Elizabeth Workman)[16]

4oz (125g) gram flour
(available in most Asian shops and some health food stores)
2oz (60g) margarine
water as required

Cut the margarine into small pieces (if hard) and rub it into the flour until the mixture resembles fine breadcrumbs. Mix in water until the mixture begins to stick together. Collect the mixture together with one hand, and knead lightly for a few seconds. Roll out the dough, in one direction only, on a floured surface, using more gram flour. Bake for 15–20 minutes at 220°C/425°F/Gas 7.

This is as easy to make as shortcrust pastry. It is inclined to crumble, but this does not in any way spoil the final product, which is deep yellow and delicious!

CRUNCHY DATE TART

(Rita Greer)[17]

Pastry
2oz (60g) soft margarine
4oz (125g) ground rice
(or, preferably, brown rice flour – available in health food stores)
3oz (90g) eating apple, complete with peel, finely grated

Filling
4oz (125g) cooking dates, chopped
approximately 1 cup water
1½oz (40g) walnuts, chopped

Put the dates into a small saucepan with the water and cook gently until they form a stiff paste. Leave to cool. Using a fork, blend the margarine, rice and apple. Knead this mixture in the bowl until the dough forms one large ball. Grease an enamel or other ovenproof pie plate and put the dough in the centre. Flatten it with the palm and fingers until it has spread evenly over the bottom of the plate. Raise a slight edge all the way round by pressing with the fingers. With a knife, spread the date mixture over the pastry, inside the raised edge. Sprinkle the chopped nuts over the tart, pressing them slightly into the surface. Bake for 20–25 minutes until golden at 220°C/425°F/Gas 7. Eat hot or cold.

The pastry is ideal for all sweet dishes; it may be used for small tartlets, pies and flan cases. Do not expect to treat and handle it as you would shortcrust pastry; it has to be handled as clay and moulded into shape, but this in no way detracts from its taste and finished appearance. Many fillings are suitable – a particularly good one is a mixture of dried apricots and sliced eating apple (complete with peel) simmered in a little water for 15 minutes beforehand.

The next three recipes make attractive wheat-free sweets, but as they contain sugar they should only be eaten occasionally.

BAKEWELL TART

Pastry
Use same mix as for Crunchy Date Tart

Filling
(Honor J. Campbell)[18]
jam (preferably Whole Earth or a similar no-added-sugar variety)
2oz (60g) margarine; 2oz (60g) raw cane sugar
1 egg, beaten; 2oz (60g) ground almonds

Line a 7–8in (18–20cm) tin with pastry. Spread some jam over the base of the uncooked pastry case. Cream together the margarine and sugar until light and fluffy. Fold the egg into the mixture with the ground almonds. Put the filling into pastry case and smooth the top. Bake at 200°C/400°F/Gas 6 for 25–30 minutes.

POTATO SHORTBREAD

(Honor J. Campbell)[19]

4oz (125g) margarine
6oz (175g) potato flour ('farina', available in most health food stores)
2oz (60g) raw cane sugar
3oz (90g) ground almonds or ground cashews

Beat the margarine until soft and creamy. Add the other ingredients and work the mixture until a ball of dough is formed. Put into a greased 7–8in (18–20cm) sandwich tin and press down evenly. Prick all over with a fork and bake at 180°C/350°F/Gas 4 for 35–40 minutes or until a light golden brown. Cut into wedges.

Crumbled up, this mixture makes an ideal substitute for biscuits in a cheesecake base, for example.

APPLE CRUMBLE

(Hilda Cherry Hills)[20]

1lb (450g) cooking apples; 2 cloves
4oz (125g) Barbados sugar (or, preferably, half this amount)
4oz (125g) soft margarine
4oz (125g) ground rice
(or, preferably, brown rice flour – available in health food stores)
4oz (125g) desiccated coconut

Wash, dry, core and quarter the apples. Put them in a pie dish, add the cloves and a sprinkling of sugar. Rub the margarine into the rice, stir in the rest of the sugar and the coconut, and spread this mixture over the apples. Bake at 190°C/375°F/Gas 5 for about 30 minutes. Be careful not to over-cook.

The apples can be replaced by blackberries, rhubarb, or stoned, stewed prunes – reduce the baking time by 10 minutes.

GOLDEN DRUMSTICKS

(Jennifer Pinker and Veronica Oxley)[21]

For four small servings:

4 chicken or turkey drumsticks
1½oz (40g) potato crisps (check label on packet for ingredients)
1oz (30g) Cheddar cheese, finely grated
½ teaspoon paprika

Remove the skin from the drumsticks. Crush the potato crisps and mix with the grated cheese and paprika. Press this mixture on to the chicken pieces. Place the drumsticks on a greased baking tray and sprinkle with any remaining cheese mixture. Bake uncovered at 180°C/350°F/Gas 4 for 40–50 minutes. Serve hot or cold with salad.

This dish makes a delicious supper snack and is ideal for packed lunches.

And, finally, one for the festive season!

CHRISTMAS PUDDING

(Jane Greer)[22]

½oz (15g) dried yeast granules
2 tablespoons lukewarm water
⅓ pint (200ml) orange juice
2oz (60g) brown sugar
1oz (30g) soya flour
5oz (150g) ground rice
(or, preferably, brown rice flour – available in health food stores)
1oz (30g) split pea flour
½ teaspoon each of mixed spice, cinnamon and nutmeg
2oz (60g) soft margarine
1 small eating apple
1 small carrot
4oz (125g) currants
3oz (90g) sultanas
2oz (60g) raisins
2oz (60g) cooking dates, chopped small
grated rind of 1 lemon
grated rind of 1 orange

Put the yeast into a small basin with the lukewarm water; leave for 3 or 4 minutes to soften. Stir to a cream and put into a large mixing bowl. Heat the fruit juice to lukewarm, using a small saucepan. Pour this over the yeast and mix well. Add the sugar, soya flour, ground rice, split pea flour and spices. Mix again. Add the margarine and grate in the apple and carrot. Beat until the margarine has blended in smoothly. Now add all the dried fruit and rinds and mix well. Grease a medium pudding basin (2½ pint/1.5 litres) and spoon the mixture into this. Tie a double greaseproof paper lid over the basin and make a string handle. Lower into a large saucepan about one third full with boiling water, placing a grid or three metal spoons in the bottom to keep the base of the pudding off the bottom of the saucepan. Put the lid on the saucepan and steam for at least 1½ hours. Top up with boiling water if the level goes down. Test with a knife, as usual and serve in the usual way.

This is a rich, golden pudding that will give eight helpings. Apart from its colour, there is very little difference between this pudding and the traditionally made ones. It will keep, covered, in the fridge for a week and can be eaten cold.

GLUTEN-FREE: THE DAILY REGIME

It is my experience that the conscientious dieter will not be too disturbed about any sacrifices made over the Christmas holiday period if there is Christmas pudding, as per the above recipe, and Hobbit Log (recipe given in Chapter 10) available for several days, amid plenty of more health-giving foods, of course.

What about the rest of the year? On pages 113 and 114, I give ideas for organising the day's menu and the only difference that applies here is the exclusion of wheat products, such as bread. If the dieter is used to having muesli and is not keen to tackle a cooked breakfast, then rice flakes or millet flakes can be used as the base for a home-made dish, with added chopped nuts, dried fruit, and pieces of fresh fruit, sunflower seeds, sesame seeds etc. This can be softened for several hours in fruit juice or milk and more of the same can be added when it is ready for serving.

There is a tendency for individuals to worry about loss of fibre in a diet almost free of cereals. Quite rightly, there is much emphasis put on fibre in the diet these days; it is a valuable commodity that we have long overlooked. However, it is possible to overrate the value of *cereal fibre*, as this contains phytic acid which makes precious minerals such as calcium, zinc and iron unavailable for absorption by the body. Interestingly, the sprouting of seeds, as recommended on page 114, lowers the phytin content, so partly overcoming this problem. Other good forms of fibre for this diet are vegetables, fruit (avoid drinking fruit juices when you can eat the whole fruit, fibre and all), baked beans (gluten-free, sugar-free ones available in Waitrose stores and in health food stores), carob powder, and wholegrain rice. As for the common potato, there is lots of fibre in the skin and most of the goodness in the vegetable is just below the skin; that's my excuse for urging dieters to eat plenty of baked jacket potatoes. Potatoes roasted in their jackets are also delicious, for those who don't wish to give up roasting their potatoes – just leave the skins on, parboil and roast as before.

PAT: Although doing moderately well six months after discharge from hospital, Pat 'relapsed' for a couple of days at the time of her monthly periods. She still suffered from overwhelming feelings of lethargy and was fretting about her weight increase which was almost certainly due to taking neuroleptic medication.

When she sought my advice about the latter problem, I suggested she cut out flour – ie bread, cakes and pastry – from her diet. I was careful not to mention any theories about wheat in connection with this illness at this stage.

Ten days after taking this advice, Pat's next monthly period started without any adverse effect on her mental health. Within the next few weeks, her disabling lethargy lessened noticeably, and the extra weight *fell* off. At this point, I shared with the patient my ideas on wheat and schizophrenia; she was disbelieving and rather annoyed. Unbeknown to me and to the family, Pat went out bingeing on pastry that day, out of defiance no doubt. She slept for most of that weekend and began to wonder. I now know that she 'tested' the theory several more times and was rewarded with a more dramatic response on each occasion.

Since those early days, Pat has identified several other food allergies or sensitivities. Whereas sampling the forbidden wheat makes her drowsy and brings on excessive sleep (and the desire for yet more and more foods containing flour), two other substances produce what can only be termed as 'instant' psychosis. The patient has discovered this by trial and error, but she is now convinced, and even fears eating these foods by mistake. As for everyone else, most are ignorant of her handicap and the few who know the diagnosis believe this was made in error. They are wrong; Pat relies on a small dose of neuroleptic medication and complete avoidance of the forbidden foods to stay well.

The above case study hopefully demonstrates the tremendous rewards which may be available for some patients whose symptoms are 'triggered' by certain foods. It also hints at the sort of problems that can occur if a wholly scientific approach is used; in most cases of food intolerance, it is usual to eliminate the suspected substance from the diet and then to 'challenge' with this food after a minimum period of four days. Sometimes, it may be the second or third challenge in the next few hours that provokes the unpleasant symptoms. This response may be very dramatic indeed, and it can be easy to believe that a schizophrenia sufferer is relapsing; this would confuse the picture so much that it would be unproductive rather than productive. For this reason, I recommend a less scientific approach to this illness and believe that an elimination diet which is not too drastic, and starts with suspected offenders such as wheat, should be tried, without challenge, for at least two months, preferably longer. Often this exercise will demonstrate the point to everyone's satisfaction. If the patient has benefited from the diet, he or she is much more likely by this time to appreciate the effect of eliminating certain foods from the diet and more likely to identify other problem areas in the future.

In Pat's case, her resumption of wheat just brought back the feelings of lethargy and she could cope with these, whilst recognising their significance. Her experiences with other foods have been much more traumatic and it is doubtful whether she, or those supporting her, would have understood what was happening in the early days of her recovery. As it is, it can be hard work trying to ensure that the dieter does not break the rules either consciously or unwittingly.

In this connection, I am often asked by relatives of sufferers if there is anywhere available for recovering schizophrenic patients to be treated with medication and diet as discussed in Chapter 10 and this chapter, in much the same way as would-be slimmers can diet at health farms. In this way, the individual could be assessed and freed from the temptation of eating the offending foods until such time as the benefit gained was clear to the patient. A couple of months should suffice to ensure that the sufferer appreciates this and the time could be well used learning how to cope with the illness and maximise individual health. At present, there seems to be no such provision in this country. However, I wonder if the day may come soon when it will be realised that an acute admission ward could be put aside for such an approach to the treatment of schizophrenia? It is my opinion that this would prove to be very rewarding for health professionals and patients alike and that it would prove to be cost-effective in terms of improved quality of life, freeing much wasted potential after discharge from hospital. It may be that the initiative for such treatment centres may come from the private sector, but, if so, it must not just stop there. With mental illness receiving so little effective cover from medical insurance, only the very wealthy would be likely to benefit, and schizophrenia attacks all classes!

Meanwhile, it is an uphill task for anyone wanting to persuade a sufferer to try a dietary approach, but remember the rewards could be well worth a sustained effort. The neuroleptic drugs, with their dramatic effect on the 'positive' symptoms of schizophrenia are based on compounds which include antihistamine. We don't yet understand the exact function of these drugs, and it may well relate in part to the food intolerance that is found in many schizophrenic patients. Gwynneth Hemmings comments cautiously: 'It is not false optimism to say at least that the symptoms of schizophrenia can be more easily and better controlled by nutritional manipulation and medication in combination than by medication alone.'[23]

TESTING FOR ALLERGIES AND FOOD INTOLERANCES

For the sort of reasons I have mentioned during this chapter, I have not included a detailed discussion on the testing of allergies. There is abundant literature on this subject which is available to the layperson. Practitioners use all manner of tests, but many still prefer the sort of elimination diet approach that I am advocating, and which I believe to be more satisfactory with this illness.

Any family with a coeliac sufferer as well as a schizophrenic sufferer should bear in mind that it may be advisable to leave out *all* gluten. In this connection, unpublished work of Dr Duncan Milne shows that in some cases the 'grain' factor is very much wider than wheat and rye; *all* cereals may have to be avoided. He reports that work carried out by Prof Dicke has also incriminated the 'beans' group of foods with this type of sensitivity.[24]

Summing up, then, a fresh, wholefood diet which is free of additives, colourings and preservatives should be helpful to any individual who is susceptible to food intolerances. Clearly, it is necessary to eliminate any offending foods from the diet wherever possible and to be patient about any setbacks and also about results. Recovery from schizophrenia is rarely speedy; there is time to be patient and to develop healthier eating habits along the way. It really should be worth the effort!

12 Community Care

What is community care? It is a phrase that has become familiar to most of us during the past few years, but what is it exactly? To some, perhaps, community care means 'they're closing the old mental hospitals', to others it means that 'they want to open a centre down the road for "those people"' and to a vocal minority it means 'not in my back-yard, thank you!'. More seriously, to many families trying to support a chronically ill schizophrenia sufferer in the home, community care may mean no more than 'family care'.

Community care has so far proved to be an ideological concept rather than a reality; a concept based on ideas that emanated in the 1960s from the anti-psychiatry movement. Its theories that serious conditions such as schizophrenia resulted from being *labelled* mentally ill and from being institutionalised in hospitals were attractive to civil liberty lobbies and to many others who were disenchanted with a medical model of mental illness. A succession of disturbing reports and public enquiries concerning the neglect or abuse of patients housed in some old mental handicap and psychiatric hospitals during the 1960s and 1970s shocked members of the public and reinforced claims of agitators that people should not be kept in institutions. Unfortunately, at no point did the reformers pause long enough to consider whether there was anything good about the old hospitals that could and should be preserved. Neither was any real attention given to consideration of alternative provision. It was, in fact, a classic case of throwing out the baby with the bath water!

The advent of the neuroleptic drugs provided the first opportunity for talking about the seriously mentally ill living out in the community. It has to be an irony that at just the time when medicine at last had something important to offer to the treatment of schizophrenia, *and because of this*, the anti-psychiatry movement was able to have a profound influence on policies. These policies are very much with us today. Successive governments here and in other countries were happy to embrace the notion that the problems of the mentally ill would disappear if they were allowed to live a normal existence in the community. Not only was such thinking popular with the electorate at that time, but, more importantly, it was financially attractive when vast sums of money were needed for the running and upkeep of old Victorian institutions which were falling into decay. In the United Kingdom, the proposed closing of the mental hospitals was announced by a Tory Minister of Health in the early 1960s and in the euphoria that followed there was media speculation that such radical change could be effected by the middle of the 1970s. In the event, it became clear very early on in the closure programme that this would not prove to be the easy achievement its fervent supporters were suggesting. As hospital beds, and even whole wards, disappeared, so one of the most positive features of the post-1959 Mental Health Act years was lost with them: the absolute right to voluntary in-patient treatment. This became more and more dependent upon the availability of beds – and these were now at a premium. A sizeable minority of schizophrenia sufferers living in the community had already become part of what we call the 'revolving door' syndrome, needing hospitalisation with each new relapse. An increasing shortage of beds was making this compromise between long-term hospitalisation and a normal lifestyle in the community more and more traumatic for these individuals and their families. Difficulties in obtaining admission to hospital were becoming common and relatives could be told by worried doctors, 'he needs to be in hospital, but I won't have a bed available until the end of the week'. Professionals were having to take more risks and the stakes were increasingly patients' lives.

At the end of the 1980s, some hospitals have already closed completely and most of the remaining are expected to do so during the next few years. More often than not, the buildings and potentially beautiful grounds are neglected, wards are rapidly closing and hospital staff are demoralised. Policies dictate that old long-term care wards be re-named 'rehabilitation' wards, with unrealistic goals set for the patients who are told they can't spend the rest of their lives rotting in an institution. As any sheltered housing resources in the area are used up, so these more seriously ill patients may find themselves placed in the worst type of accommodation. Meanwhile, patients and ex-patients speak wistfully of old 'communities' disappearing in existing hospitals, parts of which often resemble ghost towns. Few policy makers seem to be aware that many schizophrenia sufferers out in the community, including some of those who are well-recovered, are very concerned about the closure, or planned closure, of their local hospital. They are frightened they will be denied asylum if and when they need it. They don't find that the new psychiatric units can provide the space, peace and beautiful grounds they valued so much in the old hospital. Nor can they provide many of its services such as the patient's canteen, the hairdressers and clothes boutique, the occupational and sporting facilities, the discos and outings, and the sanctity of the hospital chapel. All of these, together with the familiar faces of other patients and of long-serving staff, contributed to a sense of community that has yet to be replaced outside of the hospital. Some sufferers just want to know this is all there when they need it, however rarely; others want it as an alternative to the isolation of bedsits and 'bed and breakfast' land. Ironically, in embracing the concept of community care, we seem to have done away with one type of community that at best was much appreciated and valued by many without knowing how to replace it.

It may be that nothing can now stop the closing of the remaining mental hospitals, although only a few are now feeling euphoric about this. Television documentaries and books such as Fuller Torrey's *Nowhere to Go*[1] have vividly demonstrated the misery of a new population of misfits, resented, neglected and destitute on city streets in the United States and other countries which have gone further down this road than us. Although we have been more cautious in the United Kingdom, a steady reduction in hospital beds and the gradual closing down of our large old hospitals has already resulted in visible distress on our own streets. Organisations concerned with the homeless in London, such as St Mungo's and 'Crisis at Christmas', regularly alert us to the alarming increase in the numbers of the seriously mentally ill that come their way – individuals who have slipped through the net and who are receiving no care or treatment of any kind. Indeed, recent estimates suggest that 40 per cent of the army of homeless people now living on London's streets are in need of psychiatric care. A similar figure is quoted for the proportion of mentally ill swelling the ranks of the populations in our overcrowded prisons. Even as the mental hospitals close, so there are bids to build new prisons on disused sites.

Unfortunately, much of the clamour for the closing of the hospitals turned out to be an end in itself for many of its fervent supporters. Little time and effort, if any, was applied to ensuring that alternatives in the community were planned and available before the programme was implemented. Perhaps it is even more astonishing that no research was carried out to find out if such ideas could even work. The level of ignorance about the whole subject can be judged by a recent Audit Commission's observation that:

Nobody knows what has happened to many of those who have been discharged. Some, of course, have died; others are likely to be in some form of residential care; the rest should be receiving support in the community. But no-one has the necessary information to confirm whether this is in fact the case.[2]

It is very clear that community care has never been the cheap option it was believed to be; it may not even be a viable option for many with an illness like schizophrenia; it most certainly is not an option without readily available inpatient care at times of crisis. At best, the majority of sufferers in the community who do not have families to support them are likely to be living an isolated existence in a bedsitter or 'bed and breakfast' accommodation. At worst, they are existing in the new cardboard cities or in prison (where they may seek a warm bed and food). The amount of sheltered housing that has been provided to replace disappearing hospital beds is but a 'drop in the ocean'.

All in all, this promises to be the saddest era in the handling of mental illness for many generations unless we are very careful and even now take heed of all the ominous warning signs. According to Collins English Dictionary, the meaning of the word asylum is 'sanctuary, retreat, shelter, or place of refuge'. Already some of the most vulnerable members of our society can only find this in prison. In 1970, John Pringle (the late founder and president of the National Schizophrenia Fellowship) warned:

When all is done a hard core will remain . . . who will never be capable of fending completely for themselves. No social provision exists for them, so their future is bleak. As parents die off and other relatives find it impossible to cope, the inevitable trend is for them to drift downwards to the welfare state's bottomest sump . . . discharged from hospital to nobody and nowhere, feebly attempting casual work, neglecting their medication, failing even to collect their benefits; the will-less slide to the doss house or sleeping rough along with the meths drinkers and drug addicts, involvement with police and prison, or, if lucky, back to hospital and starting the process over again.[3]

Sadly, he was right and already the last alternative is becoming more and more rare.

Recent government initiatives, no doubt resulting in part from increasing pressure and lobbying of those concerned with the plight of the seriously mentally ill and in part from embarrassment at the very evident neglect and despair of so many vulnerable members of our society, has led to the proposed implementation in 1991 of many of the ideas contained in the Griffiths Report[4] on community care. In particular, there is recognition at last that there can be no such thing without *continuing care*. At present, no one professional or agency is responsible for the co-ordination and provision of a service for each individual needing such care, so there is little or no continuity. The keeping of local registers and the appointing of case managers and keyworkers are to become the baseline of the envisaged new service. Such ideas, which imply the introduction of acknowledged responsibility and accountability of named professionals in each individual case, are welcome and long overdue. However, it is not at all clear at the time of writing how they can be implemented, particularly as no-one has yet identified this particular population, let alone its needs. Equally importantly, there seems to be no guarantee that essential financial resources will be made available by central government. Nevertheless, it would seem that at the very least there will be some safeguards built into the proposed system that should go some way to preventing so many schizophrenia sufferers from slipping through the net.[5]

Meanwhile, to come back to our original question, what *is* community care? At the time of writing it is nothing more than a variety of mixes of the sort of resources discussed earlier in Chapter 5. In some areas more of these resources will be available than in others, but such differences do not seem to be greatly influencing the sort of service that those affected by schizophrenia feel they receive. A recent Department of Health sponsored survey carried out by the National Schizophrenia Fellowship on services in the community for the mentally ill revealed that 'in no area of England was the service rated satisfactory by carers and sufferers'.[6] Another of its findings – that the police were rated more highly than doctors, social workers, psychiatrists and CPNs – echoed one in an earlier survey of members of the National Schizophrenia Fellowship that out of 889 first episodes of schizophrenia, 161 obtained no help *until the police intervened.*[7] Revelations of this kind make it clear that instead of emphasising supportive and preventative work, our present approach to schizophrenia leads to situations of extreme trauma and crisis for those affected by it. Even then these tend to be resolved – eventually – by professionals not actually employed to work with the mentally ill. Detective Superintendent Tom Williamson of the Metropolitan Police has commented:

> As police officers we can probably identify with some of the problems that families experience because we ourselves quite often get caught up in the bureaucratic nightmare of trying to refer the people that we get involved with to the hospital . . . one of the disasters in this whole area is the 'revolving door' patients because we see these people coming back in and out, getting worse and worse . . .[8]

It is certainly difficult to imagine that community care could work for these sufferers without easy access to asylum at times of need, but the Mental Health Act 1983 nicely compliments the closure of the hospitals and has in fact been described as 'an eviction order for schizophrenics'.[9] As hospital beds become less and less available and as the present climate tends to emphasise the right to avoid treatment rather than society's duty to provide it, where do we go from here? As we have seen in Chapter 6, it is generally accepted that a group of these 'revolving door' patients have the potential to survive successfully in the community if only they can be persuaded to persevere with their medication. They respond dramatically to the neuroleptic drugs but stop taking them before they have developed any insight into the connection between the medication and their recovery. Before the 1983 Mental Health Act came into force, some of us worked with such individuals in the community, giving them regular support and building up a trusting relationship. If they nevertheless decided to come off their medication, the worker could warn them that if they started to deteriorate then there would be no option but to go back into hospital. This provided a lever with which to persuade these sufferers to take their medication, whilst investigating any troublesome side-effects or anything else that might have been an influencing factor in their reluctance to comply with their drug programme. This was only possible because they could be discharged from hospital on a six-month section, which was renewable for as long as it was considered necessary. This is no longer an option, so we find ourselves in the 'mad hatter's tea party' situation that while hospital beds become fewer and fewer we have no way of ensuring that these potentially very well individuals can survive in the community. Interestingly, many of the same people and bodies who have been amongst the most enthusiastic supporters for the closing of the hospitals are also determined that a Community Treatment Order of some kind would be a violation of the individual's rights. Chris Heginbotham, formerly a Director of MIND, is reported as saying recently that 'anyone who was ostensibly well on leaving hospital should not be subject to a compulsory treatment regime'.[10] Statements of this kind by individuals who are influential in mental health matters appear to reveal a profound ignorance of the reality of life with this sort of schizophrenic illness. Surely we have a responsibility to provide more than temporary first-aid for these very vulnerable individuals? At the present time we have no effective measures with which to protect them. Because of a shortage of beds and a lack of understanding or acceptance by many professionals that the law allows for compulsory admission to hospital *on health grounds alone*, families, friends and neighbours have to stand by and watch these potentially well people sink into a nightmare of torment and neglect before anything can be done. If this is what care in the community means for some of the most vulnerable people it is meant to cater for, and for those who care for them, then clearly the term is a misnomer.

Events in the past few months in the West of England suggest that it is very possible that community care may well be an illusion. The provisions made in the Torbay area were picked out as a shining example of the sort of facilities the Department of Health would like others to copy, and since then Torbay has been widely cited as an exemplary model of community care. And yet, the number of suicides of psychiatric patients leaving hospital in this part of Devon during 1989 has been so high that the coroner has called for a halt to hospital closures until community care has been improved.

Services in the area are centred mainly on a small modern hospital unit which caters for short admissions for acute bouts of mental illness. Relatives interviewed on a television programme covering some of the tragedies claimed that the deceased had been discharged before they were well enough to cope in the community again. The brother of a woman now committed to Broadmoor Hospital for stabbing her mother to death reported that the latter had taken notes to the hospital staff which she had found in her home. These, he said, made it clear that her daughter was threatening to kill her. Nevertheless, the patient was sent home on leave at weekends and then discharged despite her mother's fears. The interests of neither woman were protected.

As a result of the coroner's protest, the work of the hospital unit has become the subject of a special enquiry. It is a sobering thought that the Torbay model was selected as a particularly good model of 'community care'; it does seem quite possible that there is no-one who really knows what this means *in terms of serving the needs of the potentially seriously mentally ill.*

THE WAY FORWARD

Can we learn anything from our short flirtation with community care over the past few years? I believe we can. It seems quite clear that a lot more thought has to be given to the needs of the people that the mental hospitals have catered for in the past. The United States spent enormous sums of money setting up Community Mental Health Centres during the 1960s and 1970s, and one of the reasons for the scheme's failure seems to have been these centres' increasing involvement with a new 'worried well' client population rather than with the patients discharged from the hospitals that they replaced. We noted in Chapter 5 that a junior Health Minister here in the UK has commented on this tendency for mental health professionals to concentrate on mild illness rather than severe illness as people move from institutions into the community.[12]

This book is about schizophrenia and as this is the illness that affects the majority of long-term and 'revolving door' patients, it would seem reasonable to assume that community care will be judged on how well it caters for them! It is, when all is said and done, the proposed alternative to the closing mental hospitals. Let's take a look at some of the vital factors that any plans for community care will need to take into account if it is to cater properly for those with the most common serious mental illness. Perhaps we should start by referring to the consumers themselves. Members of VOICES, the sufferers' forum, together with members of the National Schizophrenia Fellowship, have drawn up a Charter of Rights[13] for those who have experienced serious mental illness. It reads as follows:

1. *Acceptance without stigma*, with access to choices, opportunities, facilities and quality of life enjoyed by the population at large
2. *Information, consultation and advocacy* to help them make and implement their own decisions
3. *Accommodation* appropriate to their needs, with support matched to individual abilities, requirements and level of recovery
4. *Education, training and re-training* according to their abilities and needs
5. *Worthwhile occupation* ranging from sheltered, supported activity to open employment
6. *Continuous income* related to their particular needs and providing a decent standard of living
7. *Early and continuing treatment* to prevent physical and psychological deterioration; treatment options should be discussed with patients and/or their representatives so that they can take part in decisions involving types of medication, psychological support and rehabilitation
8. *Haven* which offers experienced support, space and privacy, providing refuge from the world during times of turmoil and asylum throughout day and night for as long as it is needed
9. *A guaranteed package of long-term support*, both comprehensive and accessible, supported and funded by statutory services
10. *Access to social contacts* through networks of relatives, friends, fellow-sufferers, churches, voluntary bodies, etc.

This Charter of Rights is particularly interesting because it concentrates on 'positive rights', rather than the 'negative rights' so loved by the civil liberties lobbies and defined by Kathleen Jones as:

> the right *not* to be categorised as mentally ill, *not* to be committed to hospital, *not* to receive treatment. Too often, for chronic patients, this means the right to live at the bottom of the heap.[14]

It is interesting too that the Charter does not emphasise the popular and fashionable principles of 'normalisation', another 'right' that can be anything but positive for people who have special needs that must first be acknowledged and provided for. Instead, the Charter implies the right for such acknowledgment and provision so that those who have experienced serious mental illness can go on to enjoy the benefits of as normal a lifestyle as is possible. The rights to early and continuing treatment and to asylum at times of need are seen as part of that provision.

Perhaps we are a long way from meeting these requirements, but isn't this the right time to take up the challenge? Unless we move away from crisis intervention to preventative care, many schizophrenia sufferers will not survive without ready access to hospital. Similarly, others will be deprived of any real quality of life in the community unless we properly appreciate their special needs. Some of the rights listed above may call for an adjustment by all of us in our basic attitudes to mental illness. Others, such as opportunities for appropriate occupation and adequate levels of income, may call for new legislation. The proposed gradual implementation of new government policies starting in April 1991 may go a long way to providing 'a guaranteed package of long-term support'. Most important of all, 'early and continuing treatment to prevent physical and psychological deterioration' would require all those working with mental illness and with the mental health legislation to understand and recognise the signs of a developing psychosis and to appreciate that the law itself provides for compulsory treatment on health grounds alone.

Finally, we know that many are already slipping through the net and we surely owe it to them, and to all those being discharged into the community at the present time, to stop and take stock of all that was good in the old system and to take this forward in our plans for the future. Perhaps we should give the last word to someone who recently wrote a letter to a Quaker study group:

There is a strong feeling that one day someone will come up with a new idea of providing a centre of caring and rehabilitation set in peaceful surroundings of beautiful grounds – in fact a place just like the old long-stay mental hospital – a temporary asylum from the stresses of life.[15]

Let's hope there will be some money left in the coffers.

PART IV
Conclusions

13 Conclusions

In the first part of this book we noted the sort of information which people affected by a schizophrenic illness need to know. The second part concentrated on ways that relatives and others can obtain help and can themselves support the sufferer. The third part expanded on the subject of achieving a health-giving lifestyle and focused in particular on the importance of a nutritional approach. Chapter 12 considered the implications of community care for people with schizophrenia, and particularly for the chronically ill and the 'revolving door' patient.

Perhaps it might be helpful at this stage to attempt to summarise all of this, and to provide some guidelines on the main priorities for survival where there are reasons for suspecting that someone is developing a schizophrenic illness and where such a diagnosis is later confirmed:

1. Seek help as early as possible and if necessary be persistent in this. Help means professional acknowledgment of an *ongoing abnormality* which you are reporting, either as a sufferer or as a relative or friend. Only this acknowledgment will lead to a diagnosis which will give the schizophrenia sufferer access to the drugs that need to be prescribed earlier rather than later.
2. Be organised in your approach to seeking help: make and keep notes about any changes that have occurred and press for explanations for them. Keep a note of these too. Remember that delay can occur before many new sufferers obtain help and there is often no good reason for this to happen.
3. If the sufferer responds to drug treatment, that's fine. If there is no improvement after a few weeks, query this. Ask if different amounts of the drug will be tried, or another, similar drug, be prescribed. It can take time and skill to find the right amount of the right drug for each individual. If in doubt after a reasonable period of time, consider asking for a second opinion.
4. Make sure that the sufferer is not discharged without everyone concerned understanding the immediate treatment plan and the

amount of support that will be available. Remember, *no-one* can predict whether or not any sufferer is likely to be vulnerable to further breakdown. Support will be needed, for a while at least, in all cases.

5. It is vital that the sufferer understands from the word go the importance of persevering with medication and the risk of relapse which makes it important that all concerned are vigilant about watching for any sign of deterioration. Sooner or later, it will of course be important for the individual to learn about the name and nature of the diagnosis. At this stage, work on 'reality testing' can be carried out as appropriate.

6. If the illness has taken its toll and the sufferer is lethargic and unmotivated, keep working at involving him or her in some sort of rewarding activity every day; not all day, but every day! If you live in an area where there seem to be no suitable facilities, then keep on pestering the local authority for some to be provided. During the 1990s, there should be ample opportunity for new initiatives of this kind.

7. Where waking up is a real problem, it is a good idea to arrange a timetable so that there is something *worth getting up for* reasonably early in the morning. Although so many find it astonishingly hard to do, it gets easier with practice.

8. Where there is persistent craving of stodgy foods, try omitting wheat for a month, as discussed in an earlier chapter. Anyway, aim for a healthy diet that avoids refined carbohydrates. Remember that some individuals put on extra weight with neuroleptic drug treatment and the sort of diet I am recommending is a very sensible way to combat this.

9. If good progress is made to the point where the sufferer is no longer seeing a professional on a regular basis, then insist on some sort of ongoing support even if this is just a named person to speak to at the end of the telephone at times of anxiety and concern.

10. If you notice signs of threatened relapse, seek help immediately and insist that someone *listens* and that appropriate action is taken to prevent further deterioration, including any necessary adjustment of medication.

The aim is to avoid further breakdown!

THE WAY AHEAD FOR SUFFERERS

Let's hope that a suitable programme and support can be provided that enables you to make the maximum progress possible. Unless you are one of the fortunate few who recovers spontaneously, the chances are that this progress will seem very slow to you. It can be very hard to settle for this while it is happening, and it is important that young people especially should not see this as a waste of precious time. It is difficult to be patient when your friends are able to get on with their lives, but most sufferers eventually recover some of their former potential and some do resume the sort of lifestyle they expected to have before their illness. Most of the latter have found they have had to work at this over a long period, and have had to be patient, taking one careful step at a time. Some have found themselves very much strengthened by coming to terms with the many problems encountered in overcoming a serious handicap. One sufferer I work with has pointed out that this can take at least several years, with improvement still being noted for a much longer time. Another, who has eventually won through and who has been rewarded by resuming a completely normal lifestyle, suggests:

Take each day as it comes. When discouraged by setbacks, look back again to the early days after the diagnosis and congratulate yourself on any real progress made since then. Keeping a diary can help.

It is very important to try not to become too discouraged and, above all, to learn again to respect yourself and what you achieve. Few of the people you know who have been lucky enough to enjoy good health can have any idea just how great such achievement can be.

From my work, I have learned to have a profound respect for the sheer guts and determination shown by many people who have had a schizophrenic illness. Some find it helpful to meet regularly with other sufferers. Not only is it a relief to be able to discuss the whole subject openly with friends who 'have been there', but it can be very helpful in sorting out any remaining symptoms (such as mild paranoia when in a crowd, for example) that are causing concern. Very often such sensations are much easier to cope with when they are recognised *as symptoms* and when you realise that others who may seem more well than you still experience them sometimes.

If you have no opportunities to meet other sufferers, it might be worth asking any professionals you know, or the co-ordinator of your nearest National Schizophrenia Fellowship group, if there are any local groups or clubs where people who have had a schizophrenic illness can meet. Another idea might be to approach the NSF (see Useful Addresses at back of book) and ask about VOICES, a national organisation run by schizophrenia sufferers, with local groups beginning to evolve in different parts of the country. The aims of VOICES include a determination to educate both professionals and lay public as to what it is like to have this illness and what sort of help is really needed. You may feel you might like to join in this sort of pressure group activity or enjoy meeting regularly with other people who have had a schizophrenic illness.

THE WAY AHEAD FOR FAMILIES

Although there is no sign as yet of any change in policies that have resulted in the provision of woefully inadequate welfare benefits and the like, families may be a little cheered to hear that, by the end of the 1980s, informal 'carers' are at last being recognised as especially neglected members of society! There has never been a better climate, in fact, for persevering with demands for any help and support that may be needed.

Many health workers are starting to run carers' support groups and professional journals regularly feature articles on families trying to cope in the home, usually without the benefit of knowledge and understanding about the particular ailment suffered by their relative. So families with schizophrenia really should persevere with demands to be recognised as the main providers of continuing care at the present time. Indeed, a recent House of Commons Social Services Select Committee report has suggested that such informal carers might be the best 'case managers' in the Government's new plans for community care, saying:

> With the greater dependence to be placed by Government upon care in the community it is time to bring the carers into the mainstream of our health care arrangements and to give them the recognition which they deserve.[1]

Many families supporting a schizophrenia sufferer would agree that they often appreciate and understand the needs of the person being cared for better than any of the professionals who come and go, and I feel that some relatives would be glad to take on this role that would at last enable them to influence the type and level of service provided.

Meanwhile, many find comfort and encouragement from joining organisations such as the Schizophrenia Association of Great Britian and the National Schizophrenia Fellowship. This is a good way to keep in touch with the latest research on the illness and on mental health policies. The latter body produces regular newsletters as well as recommended reading lists and information on their local self-help groups; these can provide moral support and friendship. Many are supported by professionals and benefit from the expertise of regular visiting speakers. A recent NSF innovation has been the starting up of a national SIBS group, which recognises the special needs and contribution of brothers and sisters – or sons and daughters – of sufferers and also their enthusiastic potential for supporting the cause!

THE WAY AHEAD FOR SOCIETY

Various parts of this book have given some indication of the obstacles put in the way of schizophrenia sufferers because of our present attitude to this illness. Just consider how dreadful it must be to fall victim to a serious illness which may have a crippling effect on the rest of one's life. How much worse it must be to be made to feel ashamed of this because schizophrenia is one of the last real taboos in our society! This is a common illness and yet the stigma connected with schizophrenia isolates families, torn between feelings of loyalty and protection for a loved one and feelings of guilt and shame that it has happened to them. Such attitudes in us all militate against the chances of early detection of the illness, as there is a real reluctance in professionals and lay-people alike to acknowledge it. Such reluctance can lead to the sufferer floundering around desperately in a sick nightmare for much longer than is necessary. It does not, however, protect him or her from all sorts of discrimination when the diagnosis is finally acknowledged in the medical file at least.

Much effort has been put into 'protecting' a very small minority of sufferers catered for under the Mental Health Act 1983 from abuse of their rights of freedom. These, of course, are the same patients who will be quite unable to enjoy such freedom if deprived of reasonable mental health. What a shame that as much effort could not have gone into improving the social conditions of the vast majority of sufferers, and into recognition of the fact that these individuals have a right to be something other than second-class citizens. Isn't it time that we recognised the prior right of a sick person to be given the dignity of a sick role and appropriate treatment before it's too late? Isn't it time for us all to take some responsibility for making sure that none of the young people afflicted by this illness have to needlessly waste the rest of their lives?

During the second half of the 1980s there has been a refreshing change in the press and television coverage of schizophrenia, with some of the media's famous personalities[2] trying to demonstrate the extent of the misery caused by this common condition and the futility of the way we handle it. This I believe to be the right approach; let's bring this illness out of hiding once and for all and so enable its victims to pursue their lives as valued members of our society.

Useful Addresses

Please enclose a stamped addressed envelope with any correspondence

National Schizophrenia Fellowship
28 Castle Street, Kingston upon Thames, Surrey KT1 1SS.
Tel: 081-547 3937
A national organisation concerned with helping those affected by schizophrenia and allied disorders, improving services and promoting education and knowledge. Regular newsletters and conferences. Local self-help groups and projects throughout the country.

VOICES Forum, based at NSF London Advisory Centre
197 Kings Cross Road, London WC1 9BZ. Tel: 071-837 6436
An organisation run by schizophrenia sufferers for sufferers with regular meetings in London and local groups evolving in various parts of the UK.

Schizophrenia Association of Great Britain
International Schizophrenia Centre, Bryn Hyfryd, The Crescent, Bangor, Gwynedd, LL57 2AG. Tel: 0248 354048
A national organisation actively involved in research to find a biochemical cause and a cure for this illness. Provides a newsletter and up-dates on exciting work sponsored by the association at Bangor University.

SANE, Schizophrenia: A National Emergency
6th Floor, 120 Regent Street, London W1A 5FE
An organisation which raises funds for research and, on a smaller scale, for community projects. Campaigns to raise awareness of the problems caused by schizophrenia and for better care for sufferers and relatives.

MIND (National Association for Mental Health)
22 Harley Street, London, W1N 2ED
Involved in all matters concerning mental illness and mental handicap.
Local groups organise drop-in centres, group homes and other facilities.

Disability Alliance
25 Denmark Street, London WC2H 8NJ. Tel: 071-240 0806
Publishes the best and most comprehensive handbook on benefits and
allowances for the disabled, updated annually.

Further Reading

Books already recommended in the text are not included in this list.

Schizophrenia at Home: Clare Creer and John Wing (NSF, second edition, 1988).

The Forgotten Illness: Marjorie Wallace, a collection of the award-winning series of articles published in *The Times* during December 1985 and some of the abundant correspondence that followed.

Slipping through the Net: (NSF, 1989).

The above three publications are available from the National Schizophrenia Fellowship (see Useful Addresses).

Surviving Schizophrenia: E. Fuller Torrey (Harper & Row, New York, 1983). Despite a confusing reference system, this book is probably the most comprehensive and sensible coverage of schizophrenia available, and is also very readable.

Welcome Silence: Carol North, MD (Simon & Schuster, 1988). A dramatic and personal account of what it is like to have a long and severe schizophrenic illness, by a recovered sufferer who is now a practising psychiatrist.

Stanley and the Women: Kingsley Amis. A humorous yet moving novel which brilliantly demonstrates the shortcomings of a 'family theory' approach to schizophrenia.

Gluten-free Cooking: Rita Greer (Thorsons Publishers Ltd, 1978).

The Allergy Diet: E. Workman, Dr John Hunter and Dr Virginia Alun Jones (Positive Health Guide, Martin Dunitz, 1984).

Wheatless Cooking: Lynette Coffey (David & Charles, 1985).

The last three books are available in health food stores and booksellers and contain useful recipes for anyone attempting a wheat-gluten-free diet.

References

Chapter 1

1. T. J. Crow, *British Journal of Psychiatry*, 137, pp383–6 (1980).
2. Derek Richter, *Research in Mental Illness*, p86 (Wm Heinemann Medical Books Ltd, 1984).
3. A. Hoffer, in *Medical Applications of Clinical Nutrition*, ed Jeffrey Bland, PhD, copyright © 1983 by Keats Publishing Inc; reprinted by permission of Keats Publishing Inc, New Canaan, CT.
4. See 2 above, p105.
5. See 2 above, p105, quoting J. L. Karlsson, 'Genetic basis of intellectual variation in Iceland', *Hereditas*, 195, pp283–8 (1981).
6. Carter and Watts, 'Possible biological advantages among schizophrenics' relatives', *British Journal of Psychiatry*, 118, pp453–60 (1971).
7. *Schizophrenia*, NSF publication (1985); these figures are published by kind permission of the National Schizophrenia Fellowship.
8. What Is the National Schizophrenia Fellowship?, NSF publicity leaflet; this extract is published by kind permission of the National Schizophrenia Fellowship.

Chapter 3

1. S. S. Kety, in 'Rationalization to reason', *American Journal of Psychiatry*, 131, pp957–63 (1974).
2. F. J. Kallman, *The Genetics of Schizophrenia* (J. J. Augustin, Locust Valley, NY 1938).
3. F. J. Kallman, 'The genetic theory of schizophrenia: an analysis of 691 schizophrenic twin index families', *American Journal of Psychiatry*, 103, pp309–22 (1946).
4. E. Slater, *Psychotic and neurotic illnesses in twins* (HMSO, London, 1953).
5. L. L. Heston, 'Psychiatric disorders in foster home reared children of schizophrenic mothers', *British Journal of Medicine*, 112, pp819–25 (1966).
6. Rosenthal et al, 'The adopted away offspring of schizophrenics', *American Journal of Psychiatry*, 128, pp307–11 (1971).
7. Kety et al, 'Mental illness in the biological and adoptive families of adopted schizophrenics', *American Journal of Psychiatry*, 128, pp82–6 (1971).
8. Wender et al, 'Social class and psychopathology in adoptees: a natural experimental method for separating the roles of genetic and experiential factors', *Archives of General Psychiatry*, 28, pp318–25 (1973).
9. Wender et al, 'Crossfostering: a research strategy for clarifying the role of

genetic and experiential factors in the etiology of schizophrenics', *Archives of General Psychiatry*, 30, pp121–8 (1974).

10. F. C. Dohan, 'Cereals and schizophrenia: data and hypothesis', *Acta Psychiatrica Scandinavica*, 42, pp125–52 (1966).

11. F. Fromm-Reichmann, 'Notes on the development of treatment of schizophrenics by psychoanalytic psychotherapy', *Psychiatry*, 11, pp263–73 (1948).

12. Bateson et al, 'Toward a theory of schizophrenia', *Behavioral Science*, 1, pp251–64 (1956).

13. Wynne and Singer, 'Thought disorder and family relations of schizophrenics, I: A research strategy', *Archives of General Psychiatry*, pp191–8 (1963).

14. Wynne and Singer, 'Thought disorder and family relations of schizophrenics, II: A classification of forms of thinking', *Archives of General Psychiatry*, 9, pp199–206 (1963).

15. J. H. Liem, 'Effects of verbal communications of parents and children: a comparison of normal and schizophrenic families', *Journal of Consulting and Clinical Psychology*, 42, pp438–50 (1974).

16. John Pringle, OBE, article in *The Times*, 'A case of schizophrenia' (9 May 1970); © Times Newspapers Ltd.

17. Neale and Oltmanns, *Schizophrenia*, p339 (John Wiley & Sons, 1980); copyright © John Wiley & Sons, Inc.

18. A. Hoffer, in *Medical Applications of Clinical Nutrition*, ed Jeffrey Bland, PhD, copyright © 1983 by Keats Publishing Inc; reprinted by permission of Keats Publishing Inc, New Canaan, CT.

19. Pfeiffer and Aston, *The Golden Pamphlet* (Princeton Brain Bio Centre, 1980).

20. Frohman et al, 'Evidence of a plasma factor in schizophrenia', *Archives of General Psychiatry*, 2, pp263–7 (1960).

21. Bergen et al, 'Taraxein-like extracts: effects on rat behaviour', *Archives of General Psychiatry*, 12, pp80–2 (1985).

22. L. Bender, 'Childhood schizophrenia', *Psychiatric Quarterly*, 27, pp663–81 (1953).

23. Graff and Handford, 'Coeliac syndrome in the case histories of five schizophrenics', *Psychiatric Quarterly*, 35, pp306–13 (1961).

24. Dohan et al, 'Relapsed schizophrenics: more rapid improvement on a milk- and cereal-free diet', *British Journal of Psychiatry*, 115, pp595–6 (1969).

25. Dohan and Grasberger, 'Relapsed schizophrenics: earlier discharge from the hospital after cereal-free, milk-free diet', *American Journal of Psychiatry*, 130, pp685–8 (1973).

26. Singh and Kay, 'Wheat gluten as a pathogenic factor in schizophrenia', *Science*, 191, pp401–2 (1976).

27. D. S. King, 'Statistical power of the controlled research on wheat gluten and schizophrenia', *Biological Psychiatry*, 1985, 20: pp785–7.

28. Hugh Gurling and colleagues, Middlesex Hospital, research results reported in NATURE, 10th November 1988.

29. S. A. Mednick et al, 'Prospective Longitudinal Research', published on behalf of World Health Organisation Regional Office for Europe by Oxford

University Press, 1981
30. Parnas et al, 'Perinatal Complications and Clinical Outcome within the Schizophrenic Spectrum', *British Journal of Psychiatry*, 140, pp416–420 (1982b).
31. Woerner et al, 'Pregnancy and Birth Complications in Psychiatric Patients; a comparison of schizophrenic and personality disorder patients with their siblings', *Acta Psychiatrica Scandinavica*, 49, pp712–721 (1973).
32. Stabenau and Pollin, 'Early Characteristics of Monozygotic Twins Discordant for Schizophrenia', *Archives of General Psychiatry*, 17, pp723–734 (1967).

Chapter 4
 1. Green and Costain, *Pharmacology and Biochemistry of Psychiatric Disorders* p114 (John Wiley & Sons, 1981); copyright © 1981 John Wiley & Sons Ltd.
 2. *British National Formulary*, 10, p139 (1985), a joint publication of the British Medical Association and the Pharmaceutical Society of Great Britain; editorial office 1 Lambeth High Street, London, SE1 7JN; reproduced by permission.
 3. Neale and Oltmanns, *Schizophrenia*, p423 (John Wiley & Sons Ltd, 1980); copyright © 1980 John Wiley & Sons Inc.
 4. G. W. Brown, 'Experiences of discharged chronic schizophrenic patients in various types of living groups', *Millbank Memorial Fund Quarterly*, 37, p105 (1959).
 5. Brown et al, *Schizophrenia and Social Care* (Maudsley Monograph No 17, 1966).
 6. Vaughn and Leff, 'The influence of family and social factors on the course of psychiatric illness: a comparison of schizophrenic and depressed neurotic patients', *British Journal of Psychiatry*, 129, pp125–37 (1976).
 7. See 1 above, p108.
 8. Don Young, Schizophrenia Association of Great Britain newsletter (June 1985).
 9. Derek Richter, *Research in Mental Illness*, p86 (Wm Heinemann Medical Books Ltd, 1984).
10. See 6 above.
11. J. K. Wing, *Schizophrenia and its Management in the Community*, p18, published by the NSF from an article published in *Psychiatric Medicine*, New York, 1977; this extract is published by kind permission of the National Schizophrenia Fellowship and the author.
12. See 11 above, p28.
13. Gwynneth Hemmings, Schizophrenia Association of Great Britain newsletter (June 1980).
14. J. F. MacMillan and colleagues, 'Expressed Emotion and Relapse', *British Journal of Psychiatry*, 148, pp133–43 (1986).
15. See 14 above.
16. Northwick Park Study of First Episodes of Schizophrenia, Parts I–IV, *British Journal of Psychiatry*, 148, pp115–43 (1986).

Chapter 5

1. *Schizophrenia*, NSF publication (1985); this extract is published by permission of the National Schizophrenia Fellowship.
2. Jackie Ferris and Faye Wilson, excerpt from *Schizophrenia – opening the door, Social Work Today* – 27 October 1988.
3. Edwina Currie at 1988 Annual MIND Conference, reported in *Social Work Today*, 27 October 1988.
4. Mary Tyler – unpublished survey of members of National Schizophrenia Fellowship (1988). Quoted by permission of Mary Tyler.
5. Report on Primary Health Care in Inner London (1981) by Study Group chaired by Professor Acheson.
6. *Mental Hospital Closures* published by NSF in association with SANE (Schizophrenia: A National Emergency), p10, reprinted with permission of NSF and SANE.
7. For example, Max Birchwood and his colleagues at All Saints Hospital in Birmingham, and Liz Kuipers at the Institute of Psychiatry in London.
8. See CCETSW Paper 19.25 – *Refresher Training for ASWs* – February 1990.
9. Edwina Currie at Question Time in the House of Commons, reported in *Social Work Today*, 5 May 1988.
10. At Southampton various types of sheltered accommodation have been made available which allow for gradual progress to more independent living within a supported situation.
11. *Schizophrenia*, P3, NSF publication (1985). This extract is reprinted by permission of the National Schizophrenia Fellowship.
12. DSS leaflet NI. 205.
13. Dept of Health letter ref PL/OC(89)12, 3 November 1989.
14. C. Greer and J. Wing – *Schizophrenia at Home* (1974), p47; this extract is reprinted by permission of the National Schizophrenia Fellowship and the authors.

Chapter 6

1. *Schizophrenia*, NSF publication (1985); this extract is reprinted by kind permission of the National Schizophrenia Fellowship.
2. Mental Health Act 1983, p2 (HMSO, London).
3. See 2 above, p3.
4. See 2 above, p23.
5. See 2 above, p12.
6. Larry Gostin, *A Practical Guide to Mental Health Law*, p26 (MIND, 1983).
7. See 6 above, p26.

Chapter 7

1. See E. Fuller Torrey, MD, *Surviving Schizophrenia*, p66, Harper & Row, 1983.
2. See E. Slater and M. Roth, *Clinical Psychiatry*, p308 and p311, 3rd edition, published by Balliere Tindell, London, 1977.

3. See discussion on p115 of (1) above.

Chapter 9

1. J. K. Wing, *Schizophrenia and its Management in the Community*, p18, published by NSF from an article published in *Psychiatric Medicine*, New York (1977); this extract is published by kind permission of National Schizophrenia Fellowship and the author.
2. 'Life After Mental Illness?', title of national MIND conference 1984.
3. K. Cooper, *Aerobics* (Bantam Books, 1968).
4. Thaddeus Kostrubala, *The Joy of Running* (Lippincott, 1976).

Chapter 10

1. Maurice Hanssen, with Jill Marsden, *E for Additives* (Thorsons, 1984).
2. Caroline Walker and Geoffrey Cannon, *The Food Scandal* (Century Publishing, 1984).
3. Health Education Council, NACNE Report (1983).
4. Richard J. Wurtman, *Nutrients That Modify Brain Function*, paper (Massachusetts Institute of Technology).
5. See 4 above.
6. Patrick Holford, information leaflet, Institute for Optimum Nutrition.
7. D. Cooper and C. Pfeiffer, *Functional Hypoglycaemia: Ubiquitous Malady*, paper (Brain Bio Centre, Princeton, New Jersey).
8. William H. Philpott, MD, and Dwight K. Kalita, PhD, *Brain Allergies*, p118; copyright © 1980 Dwight K. Kalita and William H. Philpott; reprinted by permission of Keats Publishing Inc, New Canaan, CT.
9. Patrick Holford, *Vitamin Vitality* (Collins, 1985).
10. Patrick Holford, *The Whole Health Manual* (Thorsons, 1983).
11. Leslie and Susannah Kenton, *Raw Energy* (Century Publishing, 1984).
12. David Canter, Kay Canter and Daphne Swann, *The Cranks Recipe Book* (Panther, Granada Publishing, 1985).
13. Veronica Oxley and Jennifer Pinker, *The Sugar-Free Cookbook* (Lansdowne Press, Australia, 1981); reprinted by permission of the authors.
14. A. Hoffer, *Orthomolecular Treatment of Schizophrenia*, Society for Environmental Therapy newsletter, 4, 3 (September 1984).
15. See 11 above, p115; reprinted by permission of the publishers.
16. *Optimum Nutrition*, journal published by the Institute for Optimum Nutrition, 1, 4, p28, autumn 1985.

Chapter 11

1. Fabienne Smith, Society for Environmental Therapy newsletter, 4, 3, p9 (December 1983).
2. *Food Intolerance and Food Aversion*, p4, Royal College of Physicians and British Nutrition Foundation (1984).
3. L. Bender, 'Childhood Schizophrenia', *Psychiatric Quarterly*, 27, pp003–081 (1953).

4. H. Graff and A. Handford, 'Coeliac syndrome in the case histories of five schizophrenics', *Psychiatric Quarterly*, 35, pp306–13 (1965).
5. F. C. Dohan, 'Cereals and Schizophrenia Data and Hypothesis' (Dept of Medicine, School of Medicine, University of Pennsylvania, Philadelphia, and the Veterans Administration Hospital, Coatesville, Pennsylvania, USA).
6. F. C. Dohan, 'Cereals and schizophrenia data and hypothesis', *Acta Psychiatrica Scandinavica*, 42, pp125–52 (1966).
7. F. C. Dohan, 'Schizophrenia and neuroactive peptides from food', *The Lancet* (12 May 1979).
8. F. C. Dohan, J. C. Grasberger et al, 'Relapsed schizophrenics: more rapid improvement on a milk- and cereal-free diet', *British Journal of Psychiatry*, 115, pp595–6 (1969).
9. M. M. Singh and S. R. Kay, 'Wheat Gluten as a Pathogenic Factor in Schizophrenia', *Science*, 191, p401 (1976).
10. C. Pfeiffer, lecture, Institute of Optimum Nutrition, London (April 1984).
11. W. A. Hemmings, 'The entry into the brain of large molecules derived from dietary protein', Proceedings of the Royal Society.
12. C. Zioudrou, R. A. Streaty and W. A. Klee, 'Opioid peptides derived from food proteins: the exorphins', *Journal of Biological Chemistry*, 254, pp2446–9 (1979).
13. V. Rippere, *The Allergy Problem: Why People Suffer and What Should Be Done* (Thorsons, 1983).
14. See, for example, *The Allergy Diet*, by E. Workman, J. Hunter and V. Alun Jones (Positive Health Guide, Martin Dunitz, 1984).
15. Honor J. Campbell, *The Foodwatch Alternative Cook-book* (Foodwatch, Butts Pond Industrial Estate, Sturminster Newton, Dorset).
16. See 14 above, p95.
17. Rita Greer, *Gluten-Free Cooking*, p72 (Thorsons, 1978).
18. See 15 above, No 83.
19. See 15 above, No 59.
20. Hilda Cherry Hills, *Good Food, Gluten Free*, p99 (Roberts Publications, 225 Putney Bridge Road, London, SW15 2PY).
21. Jennifer Pinker and Veronica Oxley, *The Sugar-Free Cookbook*, p66 (Lansdowne Press, 176 South Creek Road, Dee Why West, NSW, Australia); reprinted by permission of the authors.
22. See 17 above, p76.
23. Gwynneth Hemmings, Schizophrenia Association of Great Britain newsletter (August 1982).
24. Via personal communication with author.

Chapter 12
1. E. Fuller Torrey, MD, *Nowhere to Go* (Harper & Row, 1988).
2. Audit Commission (1986), *Report of the Audit Commission for Local Authorities in England and Wales* (London, HMSO).

3. John Pringle, OBE, article in *The Times*, 'A Case of Schizophrenia', 9 May 1970, © Times Newspapers Ltd.
4. Griffiths Report (1988), *Community Care: agenda for action* (London, HMSO).
5. See *Slipping Through The Net* (1989), NSF publication which gives plenty of examples of how this is happening.
6. See *Provision of Community Services for Mentally Ill People and Their Carers* (1990), a survey for the Department of Health into the views of members of the NSF on community services, NSF publication, quoted by permission of National Schizophrenia Fellowship.
7. Mary Tyler – unpublished survey of National Schizophrenia Fellowship members (1988). Quoted by permission of Mary Tyler.
8. BBC TV Byline documentary programme, *Whose Mind Is It Anyway?*, August 1988.
9. Quoted from introductory booklet *SANE* published by SANE, Schizophrenia: A National Emergency, 6th Floor, 120 Regent Street, London W1A 5FE.
10. Granada TV programme *World in Action*, 20 November 1989.
11. Edwina Currie at Question Time in the House of Commons, reported in *Social Work Today*, 5 May 1988.
12. Charter of Rights, reprinted with permission of National Schizophrenia Fellowship.
13. Kathleen Jones, *Experience in Mental Health*, 97 (SAGE Publications, 1988). © Kathleen Jones.
14. Quoted from a report published by a Quaker Social Responsibility and Education Group, 'Dream or Nightmare – The Closure of Long-Stay Mental Hospitals and Community Care', quoted with permission of QSRE, Friends House, Euston Road, London NW1 2BJ.

Chapter 13

1. House of Commons Social Services Select Committee Report *Community Care: Carers* (HMSO, June 1990).
2. For example, Marjorie Wallace in her award winning series in *The Times*, December 1985, and in BBC Byline programme *Whose Mind Is It Anyway?*, August 1988.
   Esther Rantzen in several BBC TV *That's Life* programmes and special edition on mental illness on 9 April 1989.
   Colin Blakemore in the BBC TV series *The Mind Machine* in the autumn of 1988.

Appendix I: Code of Practice for Those Discharging Patients

Extracts from *Good Relations*: A Code of Practice for Those Discharging Patients (1983), prepared by the National Schizophrenia Fellowship and approved by the Royal College of Psychiatrists; reprinted by kind permission of the NSF.

The NSF would recommend the following procedure be followed in anticipation of the discharge of patients from hospital:

1. *Identify caring or concerned relative or friend* It should be the responsibility of the hospital to identify as soon as possible after admission the caring or concerned relative, friend or landlady with whom the patient will make his home on discharge from hospital. The patient should be encouraged to name this caring person and it is probable that the address regarded by the patient as his home will be that of a caring relative. A check should be made to ensure that he wishes on discharge to live at that address, and that the person nominated by him is willing, and indeed able, to provide a home for the patient. Particulars of the caring person should be kept in the patient's medical file, and any change should be notified to those affected.

2. *Give information to relative or friend* It is important that families should be helped to understand the nature of the patient's illness if they are to care for him effectively. The caring but misguided (and unguided) relative may do more harm than good. It is the experience of the Fellowship that disclosing the diagnosis is often beneficial and there are times when withholding it can be harmful. Once the diagnosis has been made, the doctor should ensure that the caring relative is well-informed concerning the relative aspects of treatment,

management and likely course of the illness. Booklets of help to relatives are available from the National Schizophrenia Fellowship.

Professional rules of practice as to confidentiality should not normally place the caring relative in any less privileged position than other members of the primary care team as regards the doctor's information respecting the treatment and course of the illness. Any confidential information to be disclosed should only include that relevant to the care and management of the patient. The doctor would naturally have regard to the caring relative's capacity to appreciate the nature of such information. Other persons and authorities should have no greater right than the doctor to withhold confidential information affecting treatment and management from caring relatives.

3. *Notify changes of responsibility* Transfer from one hospital to another, or from one consultant to another, should involve consideration of any views expressed by the caring or concerned relatives. The relatives should normally be warned of any proposals likely to result in any such change or transfer, and should be assured that similar information has been communicated to the general practitioner also.

4. *Warn of self-discharge* Whenever possible, caring and concerned relatives or friends should be warned of any steps contemplated or taken by the patient to discharge himself. On discovery that a patient has discharged himself, the caring person should be notified immediately.

5. *Involve relatives in discharge plans* Discharge plans should normally be discussed in advance with caring or concerned relatives or friends. The caring relative who considers he has information which could have a bearing on the decision to discharge a patient, should normally be granted access to see the consultant. The caring person and the general practitioner should each be supplied with the following information in good time:

(a) Date, time and travel arrangements;
(b) Arrangements for aftercare, out-patient appointments, involvement of general practitioner, medication, rehabilitation arrangements, etc;
(c) Procedure to be adopted in case of relapse (*very important*).

The NSF considers that standard forms would be helpful, as already being used in certain areas.

6. *Allow access to consultant* Where the patient is dependent on a relative's care, this caring or concerned relative or friend should normally have the same rights of access to the patient's consultant and/or general practitioner as the patient himself, unless the patient has specifically and reasonably forbidden such access. In the experience of the Fellowship, doctors can be reluctant to listen to a relative unless the patient is present while discussion takes place. This may not be in the patient's best interest. The doctor will no doubt take into consideration what the caring person may say as to any noticeable change in the patient's condition. Section 139 of the Mental Health Act 1983, in our view, provides adequate safeguards for general practitioners and others who take action in good faith and with reasonable care on the basis of such statements. A doctor must act on his clinical judgement if he feels it is in the best interests of the patient.

Similar rights of access to any other persons professionally involved with the patient's treatment, care and well-being, should also apply.

7. *Allow second opinion* Where the caring or concerned relative has lost confidence in the treatment, and wishes to obtain a second opinion, this should not be discouraged, unless the request is too early or too frequent. There should be a degree of flexibility concerning the choice of consultant, as recommended in the DHSS policy statement 'Grey Book of Management Rules for Reorganisation of the NHS'.

Appendix II:
The Role of the Schizophrenic's Family in Treatment

Extract from a report of the Interdisciplinary Working Party convened by the Royal College of Psychiatrists (1985), quoted in the National Schizophrenia Fellowship newsletter, September 1985; reprinted by permission of the Royal College of Psychiatrists.

Families may exacerbate or alleviate a patient's condition; or sometimes one, sometimes the other. Without sufficient guidance and information, they may make things unnecessarily worse, or fail to bring about possible improvement. They have their own problems, often very severe. They feel, only too often, that they are stumbling in the dark.

Relatives and others caring for, supporting and attempting to manage a person with, for example, severe mental illness, need all possible help, including any information which will assist them in their efforts; to achieve and maintain appropriate attitudes to the patient; to regulate the patient's regime with the aim of minimising deterioration, if not effecting some rehabilitation; to understand and meet the delusions, hallucinations and deranged logical and emotional processes from which the patient is suffering; to cope with unending problems with the patient's financial, social and perhaps occupational affairs; and to act as co-ordinating centre to bridge the gaps between numerous official and unofficial agencies, with changing locations and changing, underinformed staff, which impinge on the patient. Deciding what information to give such primary care agents involves professional judgement based on the individual circumstances of each case. However, the balance of emphasis should be on giving as much information as possible. Withholding it should be the exception; and founded on a clear likelihood that divulgence would do more harm than good. Clearly, families are not on a par with outsiders; and can usually be trusted with delicate information which should not be spread abroad.

Appendix III: Informing Relatives about Schizophrenia

Extracts from 'Informing relatives about Schizophrenia', by G. M. Carstairs, D. F. Early, H. R. Rollin and J. K. Wing, Medical Advisers to the National Schizophrenia Fellowship, *The Bulletin of the Royal College of Psychiatrists*, 9, 3, pp59–60 (March 1985); reprinted by permission of the Royal College of Psychiatrists.

One of the chief problems mentioned by the relatives of people suffering from schizophrenia is the difficulty in obtaining factual and practical advice. Many have struggled on for years, using trial-and-error methods, without knowing whether their lack of success was due to the immutable course of events, to ignorance, or to a deficiency in themselves of the ability to care. Some have made tentative enquiries but have been given a more or less polite brush-off. Although most relatives, like most sufferers, do eventually become aware of the diagnosis, it is rare for them to be given this information as part of a long-term plan of management which they are invited to share with professional staff and patient, and even more unusual for them to be told early in the course of the disorder.

Confidentiality Some psychiatrists state that they will not discuss a patient's affairs with relatives without specific permission even when refusal is due to lack of insight into the nature and effects of abnormal beliefs and behaviour. This extreme position is difficult to justify in the light of all the evidence that environmental, particularly family, factors can influence the course of illness for better or worse. It may occasionally be possible to afford the luxury of two counsellors, one advising the relative, the other the patient, but they should be part of the same team and thus be able to give complete advice. More commonly, it is necessary to help the patient, as well as the relatives to understand that living with schizophrenia is much easier if the problems are shared. Other members of the family (caring relatives) have a right to know.

Labelling A clinician may be in doubt about the diagnosis during the early stages of a disorder, or, understandably, be reluctant to use a term such as 'schizophrenia' if the acute phase could well clear up with no persisting disability. Relatives will usually accept a frank admission of the uncertainties in making a diagnosis – doctors do not need to appear omniscient. It is important to recognise, however, that relatives, as well as patients, are often aware that schizophrenia is a possible diagnosis. Many will have looked up the illness in books readily available in their local library, so that avoiding any mention of it can lead to much greater confusion and inappropriate behaviour towards the patient than providing clear information.

Whether or not the label is used, it is essential to discuss the symptoms that are likely to prove most difficult when the patient is at home. In about a quarter of cases symptoms do not recur, but it would be a bold clinician who would be absolutely confident that a particular patient would be one of the fortunate ones. The question for the psychiatrist must be – have the relatives all the information they need to cope as effectively as possible with any exacerbation of symptoms, with the side-effects of medication and with any continuing disability?

The longer the disorder persists, the more important it is for there to be a frank discussion of the implications of the term 'schizophrenia'.

Health education In the days when patients who were most severely disturbed and chronically disabled were more than likely to become long-term residents of mental hospitals, relatives were relieved of the day-to-day responsibility of living with schizophrenia. Today, without the benefit of consultation, relatives are being asked to provide, in respect of one particular individual, the same sorts of care that psychiatric nurses gave. Indeed, they are the true 'primary care' givers. They often accept this responsibility for years on end, without benefit of shift relief or holidays and with little thanks by way of statutory recognition. The very least that professional care workers can do to ease the burden is to ensure that they are brought into the process of long-term care, in the same way that they would be if they were helping a physically disabled relative. . . .

The advantages of collaboration, both with a national organisation (such as the National Schizophrenia Fellowship) and with individual relatives throughout the country would be substantial. Relatives would gain greater understanding of schizophrenia and thus be better able to help patients acquire self-knowledge. Great independence and fewer relapses should result. Professional carers would find their work more rewarding; 'community care' would become less of a slogan and more of a true interaction of benefit to those who badly need help.

Index